Stumbling Bl...
or
Stepping Stones

also by Benedict Groeschel
published by Paulist Press

Listening at Prayer (book)

Learning the Art of Prayer (cassette program)
Learning to Pray in the Life of the Spirit
The Road to Recollection and Inner Peace
The Divine Readings—Prayer with Scripture
The Divine Liturgy—Prayer with Christ
Contemplative Meditation—The Inner Music
The Prayer of Life—Praying Always
The Contemplative Way—Preparing for God's Gift

Adventures on the Spiritual Journey (cassette program)
The Longest Journey: The Spiritual Journey Within
The Call of God—Beginning Every Day
Growing Integration and Purity of Heart
Overcoming Obstacles to Spiritual Growth—in Mind and Heart
Darkness and Its Uses for Self and Others
The Illumination—The Work and Prayer of Enlightenment
The Goal—Union and Peace While Waiting for God

God and Us (cassette program)
Our Creation and Being
Our Fall into Darkness—The Incarnate God
The Passion and Resurrection
Our Healing and Hope—The Holy Spirit
Our Mother—The Church
Our Eternal Destiny—Life After Death

The Courage To Be Chaste (book)

The Beatitudes (cassette program)

Stumbling Blocks
or Stepping Stones

Spiritual Answers to
Psychological Questions

by Benedict J. Groeschel, C.F.R.

PAULIST PRESS
New York ♦ Mahwah

On behalf of my brothers and sisters
I dedicate this book
to the memory of our parents
Marjule and Edward
who first taught us to walk
on the road of life with the Lord

Nihil Obstat:
Thomas M. O'Hagan, S.L.L.
Censor Librorum

Imprimatur:
Joseph T. O'Keefe,
Vicar General, Archdiocese of New York

April 1, 1987

The Nihil Obstat and Imprimatur are official declarations that a book or pamphlet is free of doctrinal or moral error. No implication is contained therein that those who have granted the Nihil Obstat and Imprimatur agree with the contents, opinions or statements expressed.

Cover Art:

John Lynch, a Capuchin Franciscan friar entitles his painting "Guide me, Lord, thy own way" (Ps 85 1–11). John earned his degree in art from Dutchess Community College in Poughkeepsie, New York and a degree in psychology from Iona College in New Rochelle, New York. His previous works include "St. John of the Cross" for the Classics of Western Spirituality by Paulist Press.

Library of Congress Cataloging-in-Publication Data
Groeschel, Benedict J.
    Stumbling blocks or stepping stones.

    Bibliography: p.
    1. Christian life—Catholic authors. 2. Christianity—Psychology. I. Title.
BX2350.2.G77   1987   248.4'82   87-8858
ISBN 0-8091-2896-9 (pbk.)

Published by Paulist Press
997 Macarthur Boulevard
Mahwah, New Jersey 07430

Printed and bound in the United States of America

Contents

Introduction 1

Chapter I   Sin, Temptation and Integrity   . . .   11

Chapter II   Unbelief, Doubt and Faith   29

Chapter III   Dread, Fear and Trust   51

Chapter IV   Envy, Animosity and Forgiveness   66

Chapter V   Selfishness, Self-Love and Charity   80

Chapter VI   Self-hate, Hesitancy and Love of
God   93

Chapter VII   Pride, Vanity and Love of God   . . 106

Chapter VIII   Sadness, Sorrow and Joy   121

Epilogue   143

Appendix   Prayers for the Journey of Life   . . 151

Notes   168

Appreciations

I am deeply grateful to several friends without whom the completion of this book would have been impossible. My thanks go first to those who permitted me to use their personal experiences as examples in this book. I am also very grateful to our typists, Anna Cicchelli, Elaine Barone, Karen Samuel and Catherine Murphy, and to Patty Doyle and Mark Tasler who did the proofreading. Special thanks go to Brother John Lynch, Capuchin for the extraordinary cover, to Dr. John Farina of Paulist Press for his encouragement, and to Charles Pendergast who generously used his many skills in preparing this manuscript.

Benedict J. Groeschel
Feast of Corpus Christi 1986

◆ ◆ ◆

The Publisher gratefully acknowledges the use of the following materials:

The Scripture quotations contained herein are from the Revised Standard Version of the Bible, copyright 1946, 1952, 1971 by the Division of Christian Education of the National Council of the Churches of Christ in the U.S.A., and are used by permission. Excerpts from *The Royal Way of the Cross,* copyright 1982 by Paraclete Press, Box 1568, Orleans, MA 02653, are used by permission. Excerpts from *The Lord,* copyright 1978 by Regnery Gateway, Inc., Lake Bluff, IL 60044, are used by permission. "Herman the Cripple," copyright 1983 by William Barton Hurlburt, M.D., Woodside Music, Box 620-400, Woodside, CA 94062, is used by permission.

Introduction

The Man at the End of the Road

The man who sat before me was at the end of the road. Although he was young and intelligent, life had dealt him what appeared to be a fatal blow. I tried to disguise my own feelings about the hopelessness of his situation, because it was my responsibility to try to help him get through this ordeal and salvage what he could from the ruins of his work and reputation. We were both thinking—as we later realized—that it might have been easier to cope with news of a terminal illness. His situation was worse because it seemed that he was going to live with the death of all he had achieved since his own painful childhood. Despite many obstacles, he had followed what he believed was a call to be a priest. Now his priesthood was a ruin.

After months of struggle, heartbreaking setbacks, false starts and hours of painful self-examination, he was ready to start again to regain much of what he had lost. He was a sincere and generous man, and fortunately for him both of these qualities are perennially in demand. I asked him then if he could find any value in what he had been through. Were there any blessings among the curses that had fallen on him?

Without a moment's hesitation he answered, "Yes. I learned that I could not save myself—that only Christ could save me." He learned that he had believed too much in himself, in his own goodness. He had not really taken his own defects seriously. He said he had also learned to be compassionate to others. These qualities, faith and trust in

1

God and compassion, would be the building blocks of a new start.

When I asked this man if I could use his experience and his words to begin this book, he was grateful that his terrible experience might be helpful to someone else. But he wondered what others could learn from such an experience.

Many—perhaps most—people have inside them something that could bring them to ruin, either in this world, or in the next. This basic truth of life has been denied by both believers and unbelievers in every age. Yet anyone who has tried to help others with their problems knows that we all share a common struggle against self-destructive tendencies. Hidden in the human heart are marvelous capacities for good and dreadful possibilities of evil. (I will return to the story of this man in the next chapter. There are a number of things that we can learn from his experience.)

A Nice Christian Pretense

Christians have their own way of denying that we are all capable of great good and evil. Believers can be deceived indeed by their own virtue. Although Christ our Lord warned that not everyone who called him "Lord" would enter the kingdom, good Christians have persisted in believing that somehow they were "above it all." Years ago this self-deception showed itself as a form of "angelism," a pretense that the vast majority of us were healthy, well-balanced and virtuous human beings. The only opportunity to face the reality of self-destructiveness came on Saturday when one went to confession. Since most believers came from families that were intact and fairly well organized, it was not too difficult to keep up the appearance of pious normality. And let it be said that this general pretense of virtuous respectability was easier on the nerves and gentler on the sensibilities than the present situation in which confusion and scandal are all too easily accepted, as the contemporary counter-culture of sex and violence attests.

As the twentieth century draws to a close, another, perhaps more dangerous, pretense has come into vogue in religious circles. This is the charade that all our vices are really virtues. This pretense might be called "fallen-angelism." Now, according to this new fiction, a person can indulge a pathology, surrender to narcissism in its many disguises, pamper a bruised ego with all the rationalized vices and still believe that really he or she is quite sane and well-balanced. Often this pretense sustained psychology. This science which is still in its childhood (if not its infancy) is invoked because it has unmasked the pretenses of the immediate past only to offer greater possibilities for self-deception in a more sophisticated way. The pretense that one is really a good Christian in spite of innumerable warnings in the Gospels and the Epistles against such illusory thinking is simply a version of the general denial on the part of the human race that has caused so many cultures and individuals to avoid casting a critical eye on how they act.

My poor friend had learned the hard way. He had done what he knew he should not do, and had been caught doing what many others had done with impunity. Many of those who had been caught or who had allowed themselves to become captured by some weakness or defect had learned before him that they had to turn to God. In the words of the first step of Alcoholics Anonymous, they had learned that they were powerless to help themselves and must seek help from a Power beyond themselves and all other human beings.

Some Principles for a Christian Psychology

The following essays, written first as monthly conferences, are an exploration of the more common psycho-spiritual problems encountered on the road to God. This list of topics, while not exhaustive, includes a number of trouble spots for the spiritual traveler. A common area of difficulty—sexual problems—is the subject of my recent book, *The Courage To Be Chaste*. The popular response to that work prompted me to follow a similar approach to other common obstacles like unbelief, doubt, anger, self-hate, and depression.

Since I make certain assumptions in these essays and in fact in all my clinical work, it might be helpful to identify them briefly. If they fall far from your present world vision, this book is not for you. I believe these assumptions are valid reflections of the teachings of Christian faith on human nature, its potentials and its problems. They are drawn more from Scripture and the Catholic tradition than from contemporary psychology. It would be unfair, however, to ignore the insights gained from my psychological training and my debt to classical writers. The following assumptions are essential to a Christian approach to a study of psychology and human weakness:

1. Human nature and the human person are essentially good, and a reflection of the Divine Personhood. They are meant to be the beginning stage of an everlasting life for the individual.

2. Human nature and each person are damaged and wounded in perception and function by a mysterious evil called original sin. The discussion of the theory of original sin goes beyond our present purposes, but I recommend some readings.[1]

3. The effects of original sin reduce the freedom and healthy functioning of the individual in at least two ways. The first is universal to all human beings and is reflected by the fact that no one functions perfectly as a person. In fact the delusion that one is functioning perfectly is clinically recognized as a sign of fairly serious pathology. The other is the cumulative effect of sin and evil in the circumstances of each person's life.

It is important to note that people are subject to greater or lesser effects of evil in this life. For example, a child born to and raised by an extremely immature girl addicted to drugs and living in the streets is much more likely to experience the effects of original, actual sin and social evil than a child brought up in a healthy, integrated family.

Yet, as the examples in these essays will illustrate, some deeply wounded people will by the grace of God accomplish more good and activate more of their potentials than those who have been born in more favored circumstances.

4. There is a mysterious factor, a variable almost entirely outside the province of scientific inquiry and beyond empirical validation, that often decisively affects human behavior for the good. This factor is called grace, which signifies its mysterious origin and its scientific inaccountability. The word "grace" means a free gift of God.

5. This gift is often bestowed when least expected, and it affects life by bringing good out of evil, repentance out of sin, hope out of despair, creativity out of destructiveness, love out of hate, and life out of death.

6. The source of this gift is a loving God, who, as even Jean-Paul Sartre came to discover, knows, calls to and summons the individual who is free to respond or to

turn away.[2] This gift of grace is offered even to those who resist it and deny its very existence.

7. Lastly, there is a loving Providence who guides people as they make their way through the problems, challenges and dangers of life. People can be wounded and dehumanized by so many forces that if they had a clear perception of them all it might be impossible to function.

These forces include such natural evils and disasters as physical sickness, earthquakes and fires; evils arising from personal moral weakness, or the weakness and malice of others; insidious and malign forces whose origins Scripture identifies as diabolical; and, finally, psychological pathology affecting the perceptions and insights of an individual, who nevertheless tries to survive and grow despite these many obstacles. In the Gospel our Lord constantly urged his disciples to trust this loving Providence, entitling its personal source as "Abba" or "loving Father."

Through instruction and parable, and especially by the example of his violent death and the destruction of his little community, Jesus of Nazareth taught the absolute necessity of trust in God, and trust in himself as the Savior to unite human beings with that loving God.

Contemporary psychology has also taught the necessity of trust, but of course it has not been able to identify the proper locus of this trust. Paradoxically the great psychological writers have revealed the depths of self-centeredness, the destructive egotism and illness of the human psyche, and then have given us as an antidote, the necessity of trusting others. The question that this poses is, "If the others are as bad off as I am, including my parents and loved ones, how can I trust them?" The answer is only to be found in the doctrines of Providence and grace which teach us to be led on by God, to be healed by him, and to help others to be healed so that we may indeed come to trust one another. Otherwise trusting others is a trap. And this conclusion is one that the deepest intuition of the human heart rejects.

The Journey of Life

Many civilizations have seen life as a journey, and presented it as such to the young. Depending on the values of the society, life can be a journey to wealth and worldly success (Horatio Alger in America), or a journey to more noble goals of altruism (Sir Galahad and the knights on the quest for virtue), or one to the most spiritual and everlasting goals. (St. Francis, among many others, promised eternal life to those who observed the Gospel.)

All analogies of life based on the journey seem to suggest that life will have its mountains and valleys, its deserts and gardens, its crises and free ways. Spiritual writers have often explained the challenges of the journey, and have forcefully contrasted the different outcomes. Of no one was this more true than of our Lord Jesus Christ, who so clearly saw that life was a journey that the first name given the Church was "The Way."

As a senior in high school, I began to be aware that life is a journey and that its various outcomes were very different. Several careers were open to me, although I never seriously thought of being anything but a priest of a religious order. Although deeply interested in this vocation, I conceived it in a rather naive way. I believed that after I entered religious life, my problems would be solved, my vices would become virtues and I would be living with an army of saints. *The Waters of Siloe* by Thomas Merton demonstrates that even someone with a great deal more experience of the world than I had could cherish equally unrealistic assumptions.[3]

Just before my entrance into the Capuchin novitiate, I received a warning that life's questions were not to be so simplistically resolved. An earnest young Jesuit came to give us our high school retreat. Father John Magin, who is now chaplain of Day Top Village, a drug rehabilitation program in New York, summed up his message in this anonymous poem which makes up in meaning what it lacks in style:

Isn't it strange that princes and kings
And clowns who caper in sawdust rings
And simple folk, like you and me,
Are builders of eternity?

To each is given a bag of tools,
A soul to save and a set of rules.
Each one will fashion ere life is flown
A stumbling block or a stepping stone.

I was suddenly made aware that I had a large task ahead. With God's help and with his tools, I had to do my own work. And I could make a mess of it all. I could fashion the biblical stumbling block. During the ensuing thirty years I have come to realize that the most important point made in the poem is that the same life could be the occasion of either outcome.

My weaknesses and my strengths, my sins and my virtues, sin and grace together will provide the stuff out of which the final outcome will be fashioned. Deeply aware of my total dependence on God and his mercy, I also realize that I must do my part, which may be simply to accept with trust what I cannot change. Activity and passivity, work and rest, success and failure all go together to fashion our salvation and sanctification, if we accept the grace of the crucified and risen Christ.

In the following essays I will discuss human weakness, and how it may be changed into stepping stones on the road to God. The means of transforming these obstacles into stepping stones on the journey of life are not limited to our own ideas or attitudes, although these are important. Grace, combined with insight and choice, is the means of change. Unlike popular books of psychology, we will suggest attitudinal changes like forgiveness of self and of others, which may ultimately go beyond the power of the mind and will. This is where prayer and grace must become elements of change.

Examples of real life situations which have deeply moved me will be used to illustrate our discussion. Finally, I will include a few prayers which capture the meaning of the journey and contain food for meditation. Perhaps more than anything else these prayers contain the necessary sentiments for successfully making this journey.

Chapter I

Sin, Temptation and Integrity

I am writing this meditation on the heights of Tiberias by the shores of the Sea of Galilee, looking out on the beautiful and peaceful scene of the Beatitudes. Indeed, this is a beautiful place—Mary was familiar with it—and it is consecrated by the presence of the Messiah. It was home to the apostles.

What has sin to do with such a place? Sin, with all its conflicts, challenges, unhappiness and guilt seems to be the farthest thing from one's mind. The answer is a great deal.

Around this tranquil lake are the ruins of several cities—Capernaum, Chorazin, Bethsaida—whose destruction was foretold by Christ because of their sinful rejection of his message (Mt 11:20–24). They were apparently cruelly destroyed by the Romans forty years after Christ's warning. It is little comfort for us to realize that had we been citizens of these towns, we might have joined those who rejected him. We might have rationalized our failure by saying that his message was too difficult, his demands unreasonable, the proof of his claims impressive, but unconvincing.

Across the Sea of Galilee from where I am sitting is Gerasa, the place where the man possessed by the legion of evil spirits lived in the tombs (Lk 8:26–39). What evil had brought him to this terrible fate? Even when you visit the hills of Gerasa, bright and green in the springtime, it is hard to imagine that this quiet countryside had once been broken by the hideous screams of a man in whom the power of evil had reached full control. The mysterious events of his deliverance, which terrified those who observed them, especially the drowning of the swine, remind us that unseen battles between good and evil swirl around us all.

Tucked away in the valley on the left is the little village of Magdala which has given its name to Mary, a follower of Jesus, who stood at the cross and the woman to whom the risen Savior first appeared (Jn 20:11–18). Christ had freed Mary from seven devils (Lk 8:1–3). Looking down on the tiny village of Magdala baking in the sun, one wonders what the ominous phrase "seven devils" might have meant in a person's life.

These examples illustrate the fact that sin and conflict are everywhere. The possibility of rejecting God and his love, the fearful embrace of evil, the devil's presence in a person's life demonstrate that there is no life so secure that one can hope to escape from sin. Sin is simply a fact of life. "If we say we have not sinned, we make him a liar, and his word is not in us" (1 Jn 1:10).

Sin

Sin is ultimately a kind of madness. It is either a revolt against God and his love, or the rejection of his law in favor of some passing or temporary good. In the lives of devout people sin is usually the latter. In any heart, however, the words of revolt, "I will not serve," may be heard from time to time.

It stands to reason that the person who wishes to grow in the love of God must struggle against sin and try to minimize its effects in the lives of others. We must all follow Psalm 119 and come to the vital realization that they alone are blessed who walk according to the law of the Lord. We must be guided by the words of Christ, "If you love me, you will keep my commandments" (Jn 14:15). But we must also realize that if we are so deluded as to say that we have no sin, we make God a liar (1 Jn 1:10). Even the greatest saints admitted that they struggled with sin and considered themselves great sinners.

The question is not how to obliterate sin or how to get rid of it forever from our lives, but rather how to use sin and sinful inclinations to grow, how to harness the energy of our mistakes so as to use sin against sin. The challenge is to learn how to love much because one has been forgiven much.

Some important distinctions regarding sin must be made. The Catholic tradition distinguishes between mortal and venial sin. This is a very sensible but problematic distinction. Mortal sin is an act of a serious nature which disrupts and severs our relationship with God. It turns us away from his love so effectively that if we were to die in the state of mortal sin, we would lose the joy of eternal life. Thus we would destroy the ultimate purpose of our creation and perish in eternal doom. Christ warned us of such sin and of the real possibility of such a fate, especially in the parables.

Mortal sin can never be taken lightly. It cannot be committed by accident or out of pure weakness. There must be a free and conscious decision to do something that will turn us away from God. This intention is often not recognized for what it is because our defenses deny or rationalize what we are doing. This awful intention usually sounds like this in the mind of a person: I know this is wrong, but so what? How wrong is it, really? I owe it to myself to enjoy this pleasure or to do this forbidden thing. One serious sin often leads to another, and it is only when we realize the deadly outcome of these sins that the trap into which we have fallen becomes apparent. It is never too late to repent, but it may be too late to avoid the terrible consequences of wrongdoing. Indeed, the psalms tell us that they are happy who walk according to the law of the Lord. But they also tell us that they are very unhappy who do not.

Does every action which seriously violates the moral law actually interrupt an individual's relationship with God and direct that person toward eternal loss? Of course not. Grave sins are often committed with a tremendous lack of responsibility resulting from intellectual confusion, emotional conflict, ignorance or serious psychological pathology.

In recent years some authors have tried to distinguish between actual mortal sin and what is called ontic or existential evil. In an oversimplified way this means that although a particular action is evil, the circumstances render it good or at least permissible. I find this distinction lacking in realism, and many fear that it may open the door to exploitation by those who are tempted to see themselves above the law because of their sophistication.

I think that traditional moral concepts have only to be extended by our knowledge of psychology to explain how the well-meaning person may be drawn into behavior which is seriously wrong and sinful, and yet this same person does not at that time lose his relationship with God because he has not freely fallen. Lack of psychological freedom may have limited responsibility enough to preclude the terrible consequences of mortal sin. The old catechism outlined the dispositions necessary to commit a mortal sin as serious matter, sufficient reflection, and full consent of the will. It seems to me that a greater understanding of psychology has simply expanded these qualifications without changing their basic understanding.

Let me give an example. One of the most common mortal sins which is seldom recognized as such is uncharitableness. The command of charity (to love one's neighbor as oneself) is a very serious commandment. There are indeed little sins of unkindness, and then there are mortal sins of uncharitableness which do grave harm to a person. Suppose someone—we will call him Joe—comes home from a hard day's work. He is a generous and devout and caring young husband. Tonight he is tense, tired and drained. His son has annoyed his mother all day by leaving dirty dishes in the sink. A few unkind words are exchanged, although the complaint about the dishes is perfectly justified. Later at dinner a real row takes place over the dishes. Now unkind words give way to statements that are deeply hurtful, open up wounds and expose buried resentment. Joe will tell his son that he is sorry that he ever had children. For a few dirty dishes things are said which may wound his young son for years. The necessary ingredients for a mortal sin are present as soon as the child has been seriously, perhaps permanently, hurt. In my work as a psychologist I have often listened to many adults tell such a story from childhood.

But has our tired friend, Joe, who came in from the office more tense than he realized really committed a mortal sin? Has he broken his relationship with God? He was provoked, even justifiably annoyed. He may have sinned, but who would say that Joe has lost his relationship with God? This is a good example of a seriously wrong act done with some awareness but which certainly does not constitute a mortal sin.

If this kind of thing happens frequently, Joe must reorganize parts of his life. He should go for counseling or do something to control his angry behavior. Failure to do so may constitute a serious sin of omission. But this single instance of anger is hardly a mortal sin. What has been said about Joe is applicable in many other situations—for example, in cases of vain behavior, greed, forbidden sexual conduct or, the worst of sins, pride. Any wrong act may be greatly minimized by the mental circumstances of an individual.

A word should be said here about the sins of the pious. Devout people are not always aware of their serious sins. When they are aware, they usually focus on a very obvious physical act which is often compulsive, such as drinking, sexual sin, or uncharitable speech. Overcoming these sins often requires a whole reorganization of life. We will consider this reorganization when we discuss temptation later.

The devout are frequently oblivious of serious moral problems in their lives because they are denying reality. This is where the prophets have their role to perform. We see a striking example of the prophetic role in Nathan the prophet who tells King David that he is the wicked man who has stolen his ewe (2 Sam 12). The prophets are those who shake us out of our complacency. They make us see that we are really worldly, or ungenerous, or unconcerned about many things for which we have responsibility.

The Gospels contain accounts of pious people who went to bed at night with good consciences but who missed the Messiah when he came. Some had even worked to destroy him. It is worthwhile considering that in addition to committing serious sins (which because of weakness do not do the damage of mortal sin), we may also be doing things that are seriously morally culpable even though we may be unaware of them because of denial.

For example, what was the moral awareness of the members of the Sanhedrin the day they crucified Jesus of Nazareth? Did the average member have any insight into what he had done when he went home that fateful night to observe the sabbath? The eighth chapter of St. John's Gospel and Chapter 2 of the Acts of the Apostles hold these men responsible for having rejected the Son of God. Yet

Christ had prayed for them to be forgiven because they did not know what they were doing.

If all of this makes you uneasy, it is supposed to. If you are like me, you may be concentrating your spiritual energy on eradicating imperfections while missing the big issues of life. You may be focusing all your attention on avoiding obvious sins when you should be reorganizing your life so as to function in a more human and responsible way, that is to say, in a more Christian way.

Can the Results of Sin Be Good?

What about the results of mortal sin? They are always initially tragic, because they place a wedge or block between us and God, between our lives and the love for which and by which we were created. But some results of sin, if followed by repentance, can be positive. Good results always require that the sin be the occasion for some greater love, one that brings repentance and redemption. This is a very important point, although it is seldom recognized.

The fall of the human race brought about our redemption because of the love of God. The liturgy of the Easter Vigil proclaims: "O happy fault that merited to have so great a Redeemer." God's love shines through the darkest of sins: the crucifixion of the Savior. The important fact is that in the midst of this unspeakable act there was a love far greater than sin itself. This is summed up by a beautiful quotation in the Song of Songs, "Love is strong as death . . . its flashes are flashes of fire, a most vehement flame. Many waters cannot quench love, neither can floods drown it" (Song 8:6-7).

We know that love overcomes sin in our own lives. We have all experienced God's loving forgiveness of our sins. And who has not known the love of another when a friend has helped us out of a pit or trap? Then our sin was overcome by the love of God and the love of another person moved by God's grace.

A word should be said about the difficult but common circumstance of being involved unwittingly in the sins of another person or group of people. The sin may be beyond our effective help, or perhaps we care for those involved and cannot and should not desert them in this circumstance which we believe to be wrong. We know many sincere people who suffer from depression and become angry at God because they feel trapped in someone else's sins.

Let me give some examples before you decide that all this does not pertain to you. If you belong to any society of human beings ranging from the family to the Church, you have been in the position of having to put up with what you consider evil. Were you ever obliged to listen to an improper conversation because you really loved the people who were conversing? Or did you decide that saying something would do more harm than good? Did you do this out of prudence or out of fear? Or did you say something and later decide that you were proud and self-righteous? Did you come away from such an experience frustrated and angry because there was no clear answer?

During his life on earth our Lord must have overheard such conversations. It was part of the price of the Incarnation. And there are greater issues. We all pay taxes to the government, and we know that some of these taxes are used for things we detest: abortion, the arms race and many other evils. Yet we love our country. Do we stop supporting it completely? Do we move somewhere else and leave our country when it needs us most?

I love the Church and can't pretend to love only the heavenly Church while ignoring or disdaining the Church on earth. But I often get angry at the Church, or rather at some segment of it. I've supported the Church when there were things going on with which I deeply disagreed. I suspect we all have. Did we support sin when we did not protest for fear of causing more discord or scandal? Do we identify with the parable of the wheat and the weeds, or did we try to take the kingdom of God by violent assault? If you have lived honestly through these conflicts, you probably have developed a bit of patience and tolerance for others. In such circumstances sincere Christians may come up with different answers.

The most painful situation for someone trying to grow spiritually is not enduring one's own sins but participating unwillingly in the sins of others whom we care for and love. It would be unwise to say that we have never been in this position because we would betray our own tendency toward denial and rationalization. Sometimes I hear a married person tell of his or her confusion because of the weakness or overpowering need of a spouse. Old celibate that I am, I ponder the conflict between powerful love with confusion and mutually experienced agony. I can compare this conflict to situations in which I had to go along peacefully with decisions which I opposed and believed were dangerous. To do otherwise would have caused more hurt and misunderstanding. How great is the pain when we love our fellow sinner and yet desperately want to avoid his or her sin which ultimately may be quite reduced in its culpability in the sight of the all-knowing and all-merciful God. The Sermon on the Mount calls us to difficult and painful abnegations, but it also calls us to a love that goes beyond sin and just desserts to the works of love. And love, as the singing poet John Denver has pointed out, is "like the ocean, full of conflict, full of pain."

Sin also presents a unique opportunity for gratitude and the love we feel when we realize that we have been saved, delivered or released. We know that our sins, when repented of, can and do lead us to greater love and openness. Repentance makes us more understanding, forgiving and helpful to others. It also teaches us to be accepting of other people's sin and zealous in helping them overcome it. I realize that, were it not for my sins which God has forgiven so often, I would be lost because of pride and self-righteousness. No sin is so great that it cannot be a help toward salvation, so long as it is repented of, struggled with and used to fuel the fires of repentance. Ask St. Paul, St. Augustine and many others.

Temptation
Temptation is the invitation to do something wrong, or to do something good but in circumstances in which it is forbidden. To be real, the temptation must appeal to something within us. It must actually draw us on. There are many things to which temptation appeals: self-centeredness, the childish need for pleasure or gratification, and the weaknesses that come under the heading of the seven capital sins. Temptation appeals especially to pride. Temptation caused Richard Rich to weigh his admiration for Thomas More against the offer for honors from Cromwell. What tipped the scales was not simply the desire for importance but the deep conviction that Rich shared with so many of his contemporaries that his life was his own to do with it what he wanted. That's pride.

The sources of temptation are summarized in Scripture as the world, the flesh and the devil. The world is really our own self-centered desire to use other things or other people without regard to salvation and the honor and glory of God. The flesh (as temptation) represents the craving of our physical appetites which can become disordered and, consequently, sinful.

The devil is seldom thought of as a source of temptation, although he is identified as such in Scripture. I have
come to believe that it is a serious mistake not to take the
devil into account. Diabolical forces operate in the world
with a certain freedom; they are like persons with malevolent intentions. Just as a mugger can disrupt your life, so
can a malevolent spirit insidiously intrude on your existence. This is not just an old-fashioned idea. The following
quotation from Pope Paul VI to a general audience November 15, 1972 was reprinted in *L'Osservatore Romano*
November 23, 1972.

> What are the greatest needs of the Church today? Do
> not let our answer surprise you as being over-simple or
> even superstitious and unreal. One of the greatest
> needs is the defense from that evil which is called the
> devil. . . . Evil is not merely a lack of something, but a
> positive agent, a living spiritual being, perverted and
> perverting. . . . It is a departure from the picture pro-
> vided by biblical and Church teachings to refuse to
> acknowledge the devil's existence . . . or to explain the
> devil as a psuedo-reality, a conceptual, fanciful person-
> ification of the unknown causes of our misfortunes.
>   The question of the devil and the influence he can
> exert on individual persons as well as on communities,
> whole societies or events, is a very important chapter
> of Catholic doctrine, which is given little attention
> today, and should be studied again.
>   Some people think a sufficient compensation can
> be found in psychoanalytical and psychiatric studies
> . . . people are afraid of falling into old Manichaean the-
> ories again, or into frightened deviations of fancy and
> superstition. Today people prefer to appear strong and
> unprejudiced. Our doctrine becomes uncertain,
> obscured as it is by the darkness surrounding the devil,

but our curiosity, excited by the certainty of his multiple existence, justifies two questions: Are there signs, and what are they, of the presence of diabolical action? And what are the means of defense against such an insidious danger?[4]

It would be unwise to see every temptation as the work of an evil spirit. But if someone notices that he is persistently oppressed in his own behavior by desires or traits inconsistent with his general personality and values, then the possibility of oppression by an evil spirit should not be ignored. The same is true when these phenomena are observed in others. When there is evidence of oppression, consultation with an informed spiritual guide or friend may be very helpful in discerning what to do. An excellent book on this subject is *Deliverance Prayer* cited above (see fn. 4).

What should a person do when beset with temptations on every side, whether from the world, the flesh or the devil, or from all three? The first thing is to recognize these temptations for what they are—invitations to do evil. Once recognized, they can be of great spiritual value, as can sins that have been committed in the past and repented of. To struggle against temptation is virtuous, and to struggle against it wisely, relying on the gifts of the Holy Spirit, is to make real progress in the spiritual life.

A helpful resolution is to remain calm and accept the fact that resisting temptation is bound to cause discomfort. Many succumb to temptation because they are not prepared to endure the discomfort of hours of anxiety that temptation may entail. The following hints may be beneficial in dealing with temptation.

1. *Get away from the situation involving the temptation.* This is called *"breaking the set"* in psychological terms.

Places, people, situations often "trigger" temptation. Insofar as it is possible, these occasions should be avoided. If you find yourself in such a situation, move away quickly. Sometimes the trigger has nothing to do directly with the temptation. For some, anxiety and fatigue can be the most dangerous situations.

2. *Relax.* Temptations are highly charged with anxiety. Reducing anxiety will usually reduce temptation. Anyone being tempted should avoid "hassles," even if they appear to have little to do with the temptation itself. The famous slogans of Alcoholics Anonymous, "Let go and let God" and "Easy does it," both reflect the fact that temptations to compulsive sin are related to high levels of anxiety.

3. *Spend time in prayer.* Meditation that is quiet and trusting is most helpful. This may not be easy but it should be done as well as possible. If you are too distracted to pray from your heart, use some formal prayer, but make it brief.

4. Finally, *stand back and evaluate the whole situation.* Anyone who is tempted often should step back and, with the help of a spiritual friend, ask what may be done to reorganize his way of life to deal more successfully with this difficulty. There may be a need for counseling or spiritual direction.

5. Someone struggling with a compulsive problem may realize the need for a supportive group like AA or Courage. Another may recognize that his situation or job needs to be changed radically to improve the spiritual quality of life. A religious sister shared with me her discouragement with her job and her living situation. She was getting very depressed and burned out. Consultation with those in charge changed the situation and

ended the discouragement. Overcoming temptation often means taking legitimate care of oneself by getting out of a rut or giving up being a doormat or a sad sack.

Integrity
The goal—the stepping stone, as it were, over sin and temptation—is the integration of all aspects of the personality. Calling someone a person of integrity once meant that the person was honest. Good motives and outward behavior were consistent with each other and with the total presentation of self.

Now integration means that the various parts of the psyche—the conscious and unconscious aspects—work together as a whole. Values, ideals, desires, and even temptations all come together to produce a person functioning in a moderately harmonious way.

The truly integrated Christian who tries to live by the Gospel is working toward being that blessed one of whom our Lord speaks in the Beatitudes. It is worth noting that the Christian has more to integrate than anyone else. He has not only to strive to be well-balanced and consistent but also to pattern his life on the controversial values which our Lord taught the disciples and which led eventually to his own rejection and crucifixion. The integrated Christian in this world is a vulnerable person. No wonder this life requires thought, prayer and the constant assistance of the Holy Spirit.

Because of uncritical and at times naive acceptance of many contemporary psychological theories, Christian integration has become a muddled concept for many people. Terms like self-acceptance, self-actualization, ego-fulfillment and many others often give rise to images of a life that cannot be described as Christian in any legitimate understanding of that designation. The Christian who is striving to lead a truly integrated life must constantly hark back to the simple clear messages of the Gospel and be guided by the spiritual traditions of the Church. A sincere but poorly integrated person is not an attractive witness to the Gospel. A falsely integrated Christian, who has incorporated inconsistent and contradictory values, is really a deceptive and dangerous model for others, especially for the young. Pop psychology has tended to produce an ersatz Christian integration.

The parable of the leaven (Mt 13:33) reminds us that the growth of the kingdom of God is gradual. We integrate the values of the kingdom into our lives step by step. It takes a long time for the power of grace to transform us, just as yeast slowly leavens the dough.

Openness to Christ and the burning desire to follow and embrace him are the essential requirements of an integrated Christian life. While modern psychology can teach some things to Christians, its insights can never take the place of the integrating power of Christ's grace. St. Paul, that great psychologist and theologian, speaks to the issue very well in the Epistle to the Colossians. He places sin and temptation as well as personal strength and grace in their proper perspective regarding eternal salvation, our ultimate goal. This goal, in fact, is already being realized in us by the growing life of grace.

In the Epistle to the Colossians (3:12-17) St. Paul outlines the behavior that a Christian should avoid and then goes on to describe the ideal Christian, the saint. We must keep this ideal in sharp focus as we work to become truly integrated Christians.

> Put on then, as God's chosen ones, holy and beloved, compassion, kindness, lowliness, meekness, and patience, forbearing one another and, if one has a com-

plaint against another, forgiving each other; as the Lord
has forgiven you, so you also must forgive. And above
all these put on love, which binds everything together
in perfect harmony. And let the peace of Christ rule in
your hearts, to which indeed you were called in the one
body. And be thankful.

Let the word of Christ dwell in you richly, as you teach
and admonish one another in all wisdom, and as you
sing psalms and hymns and spiritual songs with thank-
fulness in your hearts to God. And whatever you do, in
word or deed, do everything in the name of the Lord
Jesus, giving thanks to God the Father through him.

Is there anything that we can add to this powerful picture? I don't think so. But you say, "It is too beautiful. I
can't aspire to that. It is beyond me."

St. Cyprian, one of the early martyr bishops of the
Church, must have been equally overwhelmed by the picture of the integrated Christian. This passage is one that
many Christians may use for meditation. To me it represents a real stepping stone toward Christian integration.

All Christ did, all he taught, was the will of God.
Humility in our daily lives, an unwavering faith, a
moral sense of modesty in conversation, justice in acts,
mercy in deed, discipline, refusal to harm others, a
readiness to suffer harm, peaceableness with our brothers, a wholehearted love of the Lord, loving in him
what is of the Father, fearing him because he is God,
preferring nothing to him who preferred nothing to us,
clinging tenaciously to his love, standing by his cross
with loyalty and courage whenever there is any conflict
involving his honor and his name, manifesting in our
speech the constancy of our profession and under torture confidence for the fight, and in dying the endur-

ance for which we will be crowned—this is what it means to wish to be a co-heir with Christ, to keep God's command; this is what it means to do the will of the Father.[5]

As I searched my memory for an incident to illustrate how sin and temptation can be turned into stepping stones toward integration I decided to cite the following case from my own work as a psychologist. This is the case of the man I referred to in the introduction. Some might question whether it is an appropriate example in this kind of book. Scandalous events are discussed frequently in newspapers and on television, often from the most destructive point of view. Therefore why not use one of these stumbling blocks in a more constructive way and show how it can become a stepping stone to our understanding of Christian integration?

Some years ago I was called by a distraught official of a distant diocese who asked me to help a priest in serious trouble. The priest had been arrested for a public indiscretion involving the solicitation of a young man. The priest, who was known to be hard working and caring, came to see me at our friary in New York City. He was on the edge of total despair. Like a desperate animal falling off a cliff he clung to the last vestiges of his faith in God. Suicide seemed to be a real temptation. The bishop had removed him from his job and forbidden him to perform any ministerial functions until he underwent long-term therapy and a thorough psychological evaluation.

When I heard the priest's story I was struck by the fact that we can never judge anyone. His childhood had been lonely and his parents cruel, perhaps without meaning to be. He was sincere in his vocation, although he was troubled by a sexual compulsion which had come to light only several years after his ordination. He prayed fervently, but to his horror he had become Dr. Jekyll and Mr. Hyde.

The young man in the case was also apparently a troubled person caught in a similar compulsion and driven to selling himself in the street. His life and reputation had not been ruined as the priest's had been.

We arranged for the priest to have a long period of residential psychological treatment by professionals informed about both psychological and spiritual growth. Gradually with spiritual and psychological help the knots in his personality began to loosen. I used to travel a few hours occasionally to see him and I watched him pass from despair to remorse and then to hope. Eventually he even came to accept the disgrace that had befallen him. In the course of time a new and freer and much more mature person emerged from the ruins of this man's life.

The last time I saw him in his treatment center I asked him if he had learned anything from his dreadful experience. I recall his answer very clearly.

"Yes," he said. "I have learned that I could not save myself. I have discovered that I need friends, and most of all that I need Christ to be a friend and come to me."

I could only respond, "You have learned a lot."

"I wish I could have learned it another way," he replied, "but at least now I know from the bottom of my heart that Christ is my Savior."

Psychotherapy had been a help, perhaps an indispensable help. But in the conflict of good and evil in his own soul, he had learned the meaning of Peter's prayer on the Sea of Galilee: "Lord, save me!" (Mt 14:30).

Chapter II

Unbelief, Doubt and Faith

The news was simply astonishing. A few years ago it would have made headlines in every newspaper in the free world. Georgi Malenkov, prime minister of Russia, successor to Joseph Stalin and official speaker at his funeral, had, at the age of eighty-two, asked for baptism in the Russian Orthodox Church. A life dedicated to a consistent effort to destroy religion came to a close with an act of faith. Malenkov was remote. But the news from England was much more related to my own life and to people I knew.

Malcolm Muggeridge, long a vocal critic of the Church and of religion in general, announced his reception into the Catholic Church. He owed his conversion, he said, largely to the influence of Mother Teresa. I read the news of Muggeridge's forthright statement of faith, and then paused to pray for one of my best friends, who was ordained a priest of the Church and who now claims to believe in nothing. Is there no end to mysteries?

In my university studies I met many people who were once practicing Christians, including some fundamentalists, who had found themselves in the position of atheist existentialists like Jean-Paul Sartre. They joined the enthusiastic chorus of those who, in Sartre's own words, were "nauseated" with life because of its lack of meaning. They tried to find a home in neo-Marxism and fended off their disappointments with endless tasteless jokes about religion, about Christ and Mary and all the things they had once held sacred.

And then Sartre, the prophet of unbelief, underwent a mysterious transformation. In a published dialogue with ex-Maoist Pierre Victor, Sartre confessed the impossible: he had come to believe in God. The following sentence sums up one of the oddest spiritual journeys since St. Paul's. "I do not feel," Sartre wrote, "that I am the product of chance, a speck of dust in the universe, but someone who was expected, prepared, pre-figured. In short, a being whom only a Creator could put here, and this idea of a creating hand refers to God."[6]

As a psychologist I was intrigued to find a most fascinating confession of faith in the pages of *Psychology Today*. Imagine B. F. Skinner, the great behaviorist, who everyone thought was an atheist, saying the following:

> Much of my scientific position seems to have begun as Presbyterian theology, not too far removed from the Congregationalism of Jonathan Edwards.[7]

In this article Skinner not only quotes the New Testament several times (with chapter and verse), but he also includes this remarkable statement: "Assigning one's achievements to one's genetic and environmental histories is an act of self-denial that would have been understood by Thomas a Kempis. . . . The Revised Standard translation of Luke 17:33 puts it this way: 'Whoever seeks to gain his life will lose it, but whoever loses his life will preserve it.' (Matthew [10:39] and Mark [8:35] add that the life must be lost for Jesus' sake, and they are all, of course, talking about gaining a life in another world.)"[8]

Thus the mystery of belief. One searches for some intellectual theory to resolve such contradictions. On one side is the loss of faith, or glossing over the truths of faith by those who once believed. On the other side is the acknowledgment, requiring courage and humility, by those who once loudly disavowed faith as a superstition.

These conversions suggest strongly that believers in our unbelieving times should ponder the meaning of our own faith. We need to look at unbelief too, lest we, who think that we stand, should fall, while those who have fallen might mysteriously rise to a new confession of faith.

Two great polarities of religious experience are faith and unbelief. There is a gray area between them which we call doubt, with its many degrees. In our present mode of existence, unbelief is, tragically, the beginning state for human beings. Although children believe easily because they are uncritical, the unbelief and skepticism that are part of human life make their appearance early enough. We may speculate that before the fall faith was not necessary. Human beings were able to know God in some way. They did not need to believe in him. It has been suggested that in their original state, human beings knew God as well as great contemplatives do now. When this knowledge was lost after the fall, the gift of faith was given so that there might be some road out of the hell of an existence that had no meaning, no hope, no light. When faith was not present, men fell into the dark paganism which St. Paul describes so well in Romans 3:10-18, citing various psalms.

> None is righteous, no, not one;
> no one understands, no one seeks for God.
> All have turned aside, together they have gone wrong;
> Their throat is an open grave,
> they use their tongues to deceive.
> The venom of asps is under their lips.
> Their mouth is full of curses and bitterness.
> Their feet are swift to shed blood,
> in their paths are ruin and misery,

and the way of peace they do not know.
There is no fear of God before their eyes.

This is a terrible picture of men deprived of faith and hope.
It may seem extreme unless you read the history of war and
violence (especially the Second World War). Sadly, the fun-
damental situation of men without faith (or of those who
betray their faith) in a loving God is a world without love.
In their unbelieving world the Romans maintained that
"every man is a wolf to his neighbor."

Faith comes to us as a gift. Many of us received it in
childhood and have never lived a day without it. Faith fills
the void of the lost knowledge of God. We will consider this
precious gift later, but first we believers must stop and consider a subject we rarely ponder—unbelief.

Unbelief

There is the simple unbelief of those who have never been
called to or instructed by faith. This negative unbelief is not
virulent. Ordinarily it is not a great hindrance to growth.
We often meet people who call themselves agnostics, but
they do not place obstacles in the way of faith; they are simply waiting for God to call them. Negative unbelief is usually the result of many sufferings and misfortunes. The
believer must be patient and understanding with someone
who has not accepted that a loving God would permit such
misfortune to occur. The unbelief of a person in pain may
indeed be the preamble to faith, but in God's own time.

Positive unbelief is something different. St. Paul is critical of the philosophers and the wise men of his time,
because they could see evidence in the material world of
God's goodness and creative power and yet they did not
turn to him and believe in him. "Ever since the creation of
the world his invisible nature, namely, his eternal power

and deity, has been clearly perceived in the things that have been made. So they are without excuse; for although they knew God they did not honor him as God or give thanks to him, but they became futile in their thinking and their senseless minds were darkened. Claiming to be wise, they became fools, and exchanged the glory of the immortal God for images resembling mortal man or birds or animals or reptiles" (Rom 1:20–23).

Positive unbelief is somewhat voluntary. It is a decision not to believe, not to accept God. It may even be the result of some connivance with the powers of darkness. This is particularly true of someone who was once a believer. It is painful to admit that most of us have followed the powers of darkness now and then in our lives even when we were unaware of it. These powers are insidious and unrecognized. In the words of the old prayer to St. Michael, they "roam through the world seeking the ruin of souls."

Consequently, positive unbelief—the decision to give up one's faith—may actually reflect influences beyond the individual. This may seem a gratuitous assumption and an unnecessary involvement of something in a phenomenon that can be explained by other influences. The fact is, however, that great damage has been done to civilization and to human endeavors by those who once believed in God.

Hitler received his First Communion and Confirmation; Joseph Stalin is said to have been a student for the Orthodox priesthood. I once prayed in a church that was built by Benito Mussolini. Some of the most atrocious assaults on the work of the Church and on people of good will have been made by those who, to all appearances, were once believers. If you know people who have lost their faith, never cease to pray for them. Invoke the name of Christ and the power of his redemption on their behalf against the spirit of unbelief, especially against any spirit which is contrary to Christ.

But unbelief is by no means the result solely of a malign force outside the human mind. Positive unbelief finds an easy harbor in the human heart. At first it may be difficult to understand why anyone would turn his back on faith. The following reasons may help you identify your own temptations or the difficulties faced by those dear to you.

Causes of Unbelief

Secularism
First we live in a world built on unbelief. The secular state in modern times has generally guaranteed freedom from religious persecution, but it has also conveyed the message that faith and religious practice are just a little luxury of civilization which some might enjoy. With regard to religion the modern attitude is: "Take it or leave it."

This attitude, properly called secularism, which puts religion in the same category as recreation, is insidiously destructive to faith. If faith in God is true, then everyone's relationship to him is of the utmost importance and deeply affects one's eternal destiny. The spirit of secularism, which may appear so benevolent when we consider the fratricidal wars of religion, is a very good disguise for the spirit of the world which Christ says has no part in him at all. A wise Christian will look into his own heart to see to what degree he has accepted the spirit of the world.

"Silly Religion"
Another obstacle to faith is silly religiosity, or immature and childish religious practice. I am not referring to the faith of simple people, which may be expressed in childlike

ways. Our Lord showed much regard for the faith of children. I refer instead to an ego-centered religiosity which is filled with its own self-righteousness. This may be seen in either the abrasive attitude of the so-called ultra-orthodox, who are so reminiscent of the Scribes and Pharisees, or the cool, detached position of those who consider themselves intellectually superior. Both groups are involved with religion more as a psychological expression of their own needs or as a social force than as a living faith. Such attitudes represent immature forms of faith. Their faith has been truncated by self-seeking, a lack of trust, and a fear of making a real commitment to God.

Immature forms of religion contribute to the positive unbelief of others. Those who are weak in faith and confused by secularism may witness these pathetic examples of religious practice and turn away with regret or disgust. Immature faith may lead to a lack of generosity and a judgmental outlook, which are sure symptoms of a self-centered approach to religion.

Simony

Another obstacle to the growth of faith is simony, the vice of those who "live high off the hog" on organized religion. We are instinctively suspicious of a religious person who is too well-off. Religion starts to look like a "racket."

Many misjudge religious people because of bad examples they have witnessed. I recall being offended one day when I took a venerable old priest to lunch (actually he paid for the lunch). I had not had a day off in weeks and I really enjoyed that time in the country. A man walked by in the restaurant and said very loudly, "There they go spending our money." On reflection, I realized that this man had probably been scandalized in the past and had lost his faith. I did not feel too guilty about the lunch, since it probably had been a long time since our detractor had put money in the collection basket. But I felt sorry for his loss of faith.

Immature Faith

There is another, more important and subtle reason for the loss of faith, which involves the struggle to grow beyond the image of God formed in childhood and firmly rooted in the psyche. The faith of a child or teenager is very much entwined with unconscious elements of the personality. As a person grows, faith and its perception must grow too. This is often a painful process.

A priest friend of mine, a couple of years younger than I, left the priesthood as a result of a loss of faith. The last time we met we talked about faith. As he matured, his idea of God, which had been founded on a deep but neurotic piety had not been able to grow, so he rejected it. I could only leave him with the words, "Truly, thou art a God who hidest thyself, O God of Israel, the Savior" (Is 45:15). These are not idle words or a pious quotation. To me God has usually been "Deus absconditus," a hidden God.

The most helpful tool in overcoming the spirit of unbelief caused by childhood religiosity is the cross. A person growing toward mature faith must not only be prepared for darkness, trials and doubts, but must strive to grow through them. Doubts are especially painful, but they are often necessary for growth when an individual believes in an image of God proportioned to the needs of a child. In the fiery crucible of doubt many childish and adolescent concepts are burned away. There may follow a dark time before mature concepts and experiences take their place. During this dark time, according to St. John of the Cross, God takes special care of the person so that mature growth may take place.[9]

This conflict is expected in adolescence, but it frequently occurs in mid-life. A belief in the doctrine of the cross is the only thing that is sure to survive this conflict. It is like the spar of a sinking ship, to be grasped at by a drowning person. If the person refuses this help because he or she expects better treatment from God, then a loss of faith is likely to occur. This sad situation can be undone only by an unmerited action of divine grace.

The most important thing about true religious faith is that it is a gift beyond human meriting. Faith, hope and love, the three theological virtues, are quite beyond any human accomplishment. All we can do is reach out and receive them. The person who has no faith cannot bring it about. The one who has lost his faith cannot bring it back. Those to whom God has given a partial gift of faith cannot amplify that faith which was a pure gift. But they can and must respond with all their heart to the gift they were given.

Doubt
Almost every believer must deal at times with doubt, which is the surfacing of the underlying unbelief of fallen man. Sometimes doubts are aimed at the core of belief—at the existence and person of God. Or they may focus on the mystery of salvation and the divinity of Christ. They may involve the apostolic mandate of the Church, a particular doctrine like the Eucharist, or the spiritual significance of the Mother of God. It makes little difference, since any doubt, even a particular one, can cause great conflict about all that is revealed.

Doubts can plague a person, ruining a day, a week, or a year. They have been known to pursue a person for a whole lifetime.

By definition doubt is a state of suspended judgment. One does not know whether to affirm or deny something, especially to oneself. The sources of doubt include all the causes of loss of faith we have already discussed. Like unbelief, doubts can arise from secularism, bad example, personal conflicts of growth, and self-deception. But doubts have other roots as well.

Angry Doubt

Doubt can arise from depression, anxiety, or from both. It stands to reason that when someone is depressed, he or she may also feel negative about God and the things of God. Depression, especially when it is accompanied by anxiety (and who is not frightened by the possibility of the loss of faith?) will often surface in the mind as anger at God. "God should not have allowed or caused this to happen to me."

People may turn their anger against God. This is called tempting God, against which we are warned frequently in Scripture. But what is to be done in the face of anger and doubt, especially when they are uncontrollable and involuntary? Should they be ignored? No! That cannot be the answer. After we have completed this discussion of the sources of doubt, there will be some suggestions about what to do when one is plagued with angry doubt.

Arrogance of the Intellect

Another source of doubt is the arrogance that may arise from human knowledge. One of God's greatest gifts to the human race is intelligence, but, like the gift of free will, it is a two-edged sword and must be used carefully. Human knowledge is constantly expanding our understanding of reality, even the meaning of God's revelation made long ago in Scripture and the life of Christ.

Guiding and encouraging this expanding knowledge is one of the Church's most sacred duties. Its doctors, or teachers, are responsible for the great task of understanding human knowledge. They must also relate its development and its most fruitful accomplishments to revelation and tradition.

The doctors of the Church worked to make revelation understood (insofar as it can be understood), using the thought patterns of their particular times. This task is of the utmost importance in presenting the Church's message. It is the most important work of human intelligence. But there are other responsibilities facing the teachers of the Church in the present as well as the past. Occasionally things were taught or done in the past that may indeed have been misunderstandings of the meaning of revelation. As human knowledge grows, so does the possibility of understanding revelation. Genuine growth in human knowledge must lead to a fuller appreciation of divine revelation, how it was understood in the past and how it may now be understood. A perfect example is the ancient belief that the earth was only seven thousand years old.

But there is a constant danger in the use of all human gifts, especially freedom and intelligence. We learn from biblical accounts of the tower of Babel, the murmuring of the Israelites, the squabbles of the apostles, and the schisms and scandals of Church history, that intelligence and freedom may be used badly, arrogantly, deceptively and wickedly.

Writing to the Corinthians, those sophisticated Greek citizens, St. Paul warns against arrogance and pride of intellect. These are very important warnings for us. We live in days of an information explosion. Even professional scholars and scientists cannot keep abreast of the data pouring into their general fields of expertise. They are forced to narrow their area of competence more and more, so that they can keep up with the information they receive. This could easily lead to a loss of perspective and a tendency to under-stand the whole of life from a single, narrow viewpoint, which may be more or less valid. A sad example of such myopic vision is Sigmund Freud, whose brilliant insights caused him to narrow his vision so much that he came to deal with only a caricature of human experience.

The same problem can exist in theology and philoso-phy. Brilliant minds can be caught in a limited perspective, or dominated by a particular technique or point of view that seems to contain the whole answer. This can plunge the thinker into a bottomless pit of his own doubts. Then, if pride or vanity, which are common enough vices for us all, take hold of his thinking, his gifts of intelligence can easily be dominated by arrogance.

The history of the Church is filled with incidents of this kind. Many arrogant people made good contributions, many suffered unjustly, many had no more faults than any-one else, but the corruption of the best is often the worst. Because the danger of intellectual arrogance is so common, the Church has often singled out for the honor of sainthood those theologians who did not fall into this trap.

The blunt truth is that much doubt is caused by intel-lectual arrogance. I have talked to dozens of priests, reli-gious, seminarians and informed laity whose grasp of faith was weakened and sometimes destroyed by brilliant teach-ers who took revelation apart but never fulfilled their promise to put it back together again. This was probably because they never got it back together for themselves. They were often caught in the most dangerous of modern superstitions. (A superstition is a belief which has no other foundation than the individual's need to believe it is true.) The most dangerous superstition is that the human mind can come to understand everything.

Blaise Pascal, who profoundly affected the development of science by his theory of probability, and whose ideas are the foundation of computer science, observed that the most important principle of human reason is the recognition of the infinite number of things that reason cannot comprehend.

Theologians and those whose faith is influenced by theology must have a vibrant appreciation of mystery and of the essential limits of human understanding. The fathers of the synod marking the twentieth anniversary of the Second Vatican Council called for a revival of the sense of mystery in theology. Scientists, even more than theologians, are, unfortunately, often unaware of these limitations. When science does not acknowledge its limits it can become an instrument of evil of diabolical proportions. One thinks of the experiments performed on human subjects by scientists in Nazi Germany.

Even more dangerous than the arrogant scientist is the philosopher or theologian who does not constantly remind himself of his finite understanding. He may even accidentally produce the intellectual justification for science gone mad.

In St. Paul's First Epistle to the Corinthians there is a painful and powerful warning which those who are called to preach and teach must keep in mind: "This is how one should regard us, as servants of Christ and stewards of the mysteries of God. Moreover it is required of stewards that they be found trustworthy" (1 Cor 4:1–2). He expects the teacher to be trustworthy and not arrogant. This is how St. Paul describes a trustworthy teacher.

> Let no one deceive himself. If any one among you thinks that he is wise in this age, let him become a fool that he may become wise. For the wisdom of the world

is folly with God. For it is written, "He catches the wise in their craftiness," and again, "The Lord knows that the thoughts of the wise are futile." So let no one boast of men. For all things are yours, whether Paul or Apollos or Cephas or the world or life or death or the present or the future, all are yours; and you are Christ's; and Christ is God's (1 Cor 3:18–23).

Having looked at the sources of doubt, what can we say about dealing with them? The following suggestions are not very different from those that can be made in the case of any temptation.

1. Recognize and state clearly to yourself that you are having doubts.
2. See if you can determine the source of doubt. Have you been influenced by the spirit of the world? Have you unknowingly and unwillingly accepted the superstitions of modern science or philosophy? Perhaps you have unconsciously welcomed a spirit of unbelief into your life. Maybe you are anxious or frustrated. Doubts may come from your own life situation and have little to do with the truth of God at all.

   Perhaps you are angry with God because your view of him is too narrow. You may have thought he was a genie, a magical being who manipulates life to suit your pleasure. Perhaps you never really believed that the cross is the lot of every Christian, and now you are faced with it and cannot escape it. Those who deny the inescapable reality of suffering are prone to bitter despair when it eventually comes their way. Your doubts may be unconsciously founded on resentment toward your parents or some parent surrogates like teachers or pastors. If one of these significant people has failed or hurt you, you may be blaming God for their shortcomings. Perhaps you are arrogant. It happens to us all. You may have unwillingly fashioned a god to your own likeness, and when this idol has been found wanting, you have lacked the humility to smash it and call out to the true God.

3. The final step is to accept the gift of faith when it is given. The bright light of faith will break through only now and then. But when it comes it must be accepted. We have the painful biblical example of Thomas the apostle, who did not believe even though he had the other apostles' testimony. We don't know why he doubted, but we do know that Christ came to him even in his caustic and cynical doubts. When Christ approached him, Thomas cried out, "My Lord and my God" (Jn 20:28).

Faith

Faith overcomes that basic unbelief which is at the heart of worldliness. While it is true that every person at least secretly longs to believe because of a desire not to perish forever, it is also true that everyone has a powerful trace of unbelief. The latter attitude is the foundation of all worldliness. Faith is our victory over this perverse and foolish streak. It is, as St. Paul says, our victory over the world, by which he means not the material cosmos, but rather every tendency to use creation independently of the Creator.

Faith is a gift of the Holy Spirit, an illumination of our mind and will by the Divine Light. This does not mean that there cannot be false faith. Christ warns us that not everyone who calls him "Lord" shall enter the kingdom of heaven. False faith, an apparent belief in Christ, is really a superstition masquerading as faith. It presents a false

Christ. True faith on the other hand is a gift. You cannot give it to yourself, although you can ask for it, and for its increase. St. Peter's prayer beautifully expresses this possibility. "Lord, I believe. Help my unbelief."

But faith must always grow, and therefore we must nourish it. Our Lord's admonition to Thomas tells us much. "Blessed are those who have not seen and yet believe" (Jn 20:29). Even when in doubt, we must respond as best as we can to the teachings of faith. This means never losing the opportunity (no matter how conflicted it may be) to act in a believing way. If doubts arise from psychological conflicts or depression, we must hold on as in any other temptation. When frightened or anxious or beaten down by sin, we must go on even in the blackest emotional darkness.

There is another kind of darkness. It is the essential darkness of the intellect surrounding faith. St. John of the Cross describes this and warns us that faith reveals things we have not seen or known, either as they are in themselves or as they agree with any comparison. This is why faith itself is the greatest darkness to the intellect. For the Christian darkness is epitomized by the mystery of Christ.[10]

No one with immature faith can cope with the darkness of mystery. Fear, anxiety and anger take over when one cannot comprehend it all. The immediate solution is to slip into one of two errors, fundamentalism or rationalism. The former encapsulates faith in very tight formulas which are understood literally and which, paradoxically, limit the appreciation of what they seek to preserve.

The fundamentalist falls into superstition by not acknowledging that there is a reality which transcends any verbal formula or intellectual understanding. God and his reality are a mystery. This means, literally, that they cannot be seen. The fundamentalist is not as sure of himself as he appears to be, and for this reason constantly repeats the same formulas. These may be true enough in themselves, but they are taken—often ripped—out of context. When one is really unsure of his convictions, he tends to repeat them with ever greater force and volume.

While it would be unfair to accuse the fundamentalist of having no faith, it is not unfair to characterize the faith of some fundamentalists as adolescent. The age of reason comes during adolescence. The adolescent wants clear ideas and definitive answers. Fundamentalist preachers on television appeal to this need and to the anxiety and fear characteristic of teenagers. Unfortunately such preachers often lack the faith of children, who see and believe without being able to understand completely.

The rationalist has the same problem as the fundamentalist, but his bias is different. He, too, needs to understand, but he starts with his understanding, rather than with revelation. He makes his mind, which is a finite instrument, the measure of everything he is willing to assent to.

Many rationalists manage to believe, as do many fundamentalists, because they are, thankfully, inconsistent. They accept one mystery but reject another that may be unpalatable. Their creed becomes a smorgasbord. The same laws of aesthetics that apply to taste often govern the choice of what is accepted or rejected on religious grounds.

The totally logical rationalist ends up believing nothing, but suspects that this or that doctrine may be true. Since he has made himself the measure of what he accepts, his reality will become as small as he is, as limited as his education, as circumscribed as his moment of history, as narrow as his background and as brittle and fragile as his neurotic personality.

Like the fundamentalist, the rationalist soon finds that his god looks very much like himself. Though an unbeliever, Freud had the good sense to see that in either approach, men made God in their own image. Unfortunately Freud made sure he stayed far away from believers, and castigated his protégé Jung for engaging in his own explorations of mystery.

No limited mind, when it is faced with the infinity of God, can avoid darkness. The secret of mature faith is that it brings one to the true darkness, not the darkness of one's own shadow. Mature faith looks into the infinite darkness of the starry sky and sees there a symbol of "the depths of the riches of the wisdom and knowledge of God."

An example of a controversial issue which I believe opens up the mystery of faith in its Christian dimensions is worth considering. The mystery of the God-man, when maturely approached, brings the believer to silent adoration. Consider one aspect of this mystery which is popularly discussed at present and which causes confusion for many people, namely, the psychology of Jesus Christ.

What did Christ think? Some fundamentalists are quick to say he knew everything they know, and in the same way as they know it. Some of them think that the infant Christ spoke Hebrew perfectly. The rationalist smugly asserts that this is obscurantist thinking, and not borne out by the Scriptures as we read them today from our informed modern perspective. But the rationalist cannot be sure of what Christ knew. Therefore, in a magnificent burst of illogic known as reductionism, he decides that Christ, the God-man, knew nothing. Rationalists often seem to describe Christ as being in a state of divine retardation.

Mature faith accepts the dogma that Jesus of Nazareth had a human nature and a divine nature united in one person. This truth has been proclaimed since apostolic times, before the New Testament was completely edited and defined. Mature faith also accepts that behavior flows from the nature of a thing. If the mature believer is also informed about the limitations and functions of modern science (and the science in question here is psychology, since we are talking about knowledge), then he kneels down and remembers that the Incarnation is an impenetrable mystery.

Psychology is of little help because it is based on observation, and none of us has ever observed a person with two natures, much less anyone with a divine nature. Scripture presents some examples of Jesus' functioning. His use of the word "Abba," or "Daddy," for the Divine Being shows that he was well aware of being different from everyone else.

The fact is that we don't know exactly how or what Jesus thought or how he functioned psychologically with two natures—one of them divine. Fundamentalists and rationalists tend to present self-reports in place of a credible picture of Christ. The former think that he knew everything, just as they know everything explicitly. The latter think that he was as confused as any certified rationalist ought to be. One of the great modern theologians, Romano Guardini, has written a magnificent testimony to the mystery of Christ in his book, *The Lord.* It is a powerful statement of the limitations of our understanding of the God-man. (The entire third chapter can be read with profit. The following lines sum up what I believe to be the only intellectually respectable approach to the mystery of Christ.)

> What we have just attempted to grasp in the obscurity of divine action now presents itself to us in visible form. At first a child like any other, it cries, is hungry, sleeps, and yet is "the Word . . . become flesh." It cannot be said that God "inhabits" this infant, however gloriously, or that heaven has set its seal upon him, so that he must pursue it, suffer for it in a manner sublimely excelling all other contacts between God and man; this child is God in essence and in being.

If an inner protest should arise here, give it room. Anything that is suppressed only goes underground, becomes toxic and reappears later in a more obnoxious form. Does anyone object to the whole idea of God-become-man? Is he willing to accept the Incarnation only as a profound and beautiful allegory, never as literal truth?

If doubt can establish a foothold anywhere in our faith, it is here. We must be patient and reverent, approaching this central mystery of Christianity with calm, expectant, prayerful attention: one day its sense will be revealed to us. In the meantime, let us remember the directive, "But love does such things. . . . "

What one is by birth determines the general theme of the life to follow: everything else is necessarily supplementary. Christian thinkers have spent much time and thought probing Jesus' inner life, from psychological and theological perspectives. But any attempt of psychology shatters on the rock of what He is. An analysis of Christ might be valid for the periphery of His being, but any significance or image it manages to construct is almost immediately consumed by the power of the center.

The young creature in the stall of Bethlehem was a human being with human brain and limbs and heart and soul. And it was God. The purpose of existence was to manifest the will of the Father, proclaim the sacred tidings, stir mankind with the power of God, establish the Covenant and shoulder the sin of the world. The God-man was to expiate our sins with love and lead humanity through the destruction of sacrifice and the victory of the Resurrection into the new existence of grace.

In this accomplishment alone lay Jesus' self-perfection: fulfillment of His Father's mission and personal fulfillment were one. The Resurrected Himself points this out: "Did not the Christ have to suffer these things before entering into his glory?" (Luke 24:26). It was as if Jesus' self-realization meant that His human being "took possession" of the divine being He had always intrinsically been. Jesus did not "experience" God; He was God. He never at any given moment "became" God; He was God from the start. His life was only the process by which this innate divinity came into its own. . . . [11]

The power of the darkness of faith is often best revealed in deeds rather than in words. I have often been deeply moved by this account of someone who believed and yet almost never experienced the consolations of his faith. It is even unlikely that he received any of the sacraments during his imprisonment.

Philip Howard, Earl of Arundel, was a favorite young courtier of Queen Elizabeth I. Although baptized in the old faith, his family had accepted the supremacy of the king over the Church. Philip was required to attend a debate between divines of the new church and Edmund Campion, a young English Jesuit who had been tortured in the Tower of London and was about to be hanged, drawn and quartered. Moved by the words and spirit of the young Jesuit, Philip resolved to withdraw quietly from court, return to Arundel, and then leave for Spain, where he could practice the Catholic faith.

He was betrayed, however, and arrested. He spent eleven years in the Tower, where he eventually died, probably a victim of poisoning. Like Campion whom he never actually met, Philip Howard is a canonized saint. He clung to his faith for those years of imprisonment, darkness and trial. The Tower still contains two venerable reminders of this single powerful encounter—the beautiful Scripture quotation carved in the wall of Howard's cell, and the ghastly sign in the torture cell indicating that Campion's body was four inches taller after he was racked.

By an odd quirk of history, the present Duke of Norfolk is a direct descendant of St. Philip. He is also the premier duke of England; as such it is his prerogative to present the crown prince to the archbishop of Canterbury for coronation. Today over the little city of Arundel looms the Cathedral of Our Lady and St. Philip Howard, a man who remained committed to a faith that he heard preached only once by another brave young man who was about to die.

Chapter III

Dread, Fear and Trust

On a bright, warm Easter Sunday, a group of pilgrims with whom I had traveled to the Holy Land visited the beautiful little church of the Last Supper in Jerusalem. After a joyful Mass in the Church, I tried to prepare the group for something different—a visit to a museum called the Yad Vashem, the Holocaust memorial.

Even though it was Easter, a feeling of dread descended on us as we entered the museum and saw the pictures of the rise of the Nazi party. A deeper dread descended as we went from one exhibit to the next, even though we knew all too well what the outcome would be. We were able to experience some of the dread on the faces of the men, women and children who were shown in those terrible photographs even though they had died forty or fifty years ago.

We ended our tour in the stark memorial building which is so much like the buildings we had seen pictured in the camp. We prayed for the Holocaust victims and for those who suffer persecution everywhere. We also prayed for ourselves and our own time. Everyone has experienced dread, and we all knew that in a few moments it could come again.

Dread

Dread is a special kind of fear that grips us in the worst circumstances or what we assume to be the worst circumstances. Dread comes into our lives only on special occasions: illness, war, or some other calamity. When we are faced with grave peril that we unfortunately know all too

51

well, a cold, anxious feeling overcomes us and we feel almost paralyzed. We think we cannot go on. Death can often seem a more attractive alternative than the long continuation of dread.

Where does this terrible feeling come from? Psychologists and psychiatrists accept dread as a component of the basic human condition. Many maintain that our outer feelings of happiness, contentment, complacency, and normal fear are a veil of defense which we draw over our perception of the basic human condition, which is dread. Some psychologists hold that many people see life and all it may bring as a meaningless journey of chance. Despite technological advances, people today live in dread that life is a struggle, ultimately without meaning. We dread that our lives will be, in the end, only a collection of dreads.

The following quotation from Psalm 88, which we, as pilgrims, recited that day at the Yad Vashem, is a strong expression of dread.

> For my soul is full of troubles,
> and my life draws near to Sheol.
> I am reckoned among those who
> go down to the Pit;
> I am a man who has no strength,
> like one forsaken among the dead,
> like the slain that lie in the grave,
> like those whom thou dost remember
> no more, for they are cut off from thy hand.
> Thou hast put me in the depths of the Pit,
> in the regions dark and deep.
> Thy wrath lies heavy upon me,
> and thou dost overwhelm me with all thy waves.
> Thou hast caused my companions to shun me;
> thou hast made me a thing of horror to them.
> I am shut in so that I cannot escape;

my eye grows dim through sorrow.
But, I, O Lord, cry to thee;
in the morning my prayer comes before thee.
O Lord, why dost thou cast me off?
Why dost thou hide thy face from me?
Afflicted and close to death from my youth up,
I suffer thy terrors; I am helpless.
Thy wrath has swept over me;
thy dread assaults destroy me.
They surround me like a flood all day long;
they close in upon me together.
Thou hast caused lover and friend to shun me;
my companions are in darkness.

This is one of the many expressions of dread in Sacred Scripture. We should not pretend that any religion, including Christianity, removes dread from life. What should we call the feeling that came over Jesus in the garden, if not dread?

The foundation of dread is the fear that all we have and all we are will be lost, and that we will pass into oblivion—into a place of darkness, as the psalmist says.

This is not an idle fear. Were it not for the promise of salvation and our own eternal destiny, that is exactly the situation we would be in. Consider how wonderfully merciful God is. Despite the dread of oblivion, despite the fact that most people do not know the truth of the Gospel, almost all human beings hope that death is not the end.

I think life would become impossible if we were without the hope of life after death. The dread of our first parents in Genesis is like an overture to a symphony of dread and deliverance which is repeated many times in the Old Testament. This dread has its ultimate expression in the agony in the garden and in the events of Christ's passion.

During the past year I had the opportunity to pray in a place that recalls an unbelievable dread. Near the oldest part of Jerusalem, the city of David, is a beautiful French church called St. Peter in Galicantu, which is built on the foundations of the house of Caiaphas the high priest. Below the church is a stone cistern which was once a dungeon. Our Lord was probably held there the night before his crucifixion. Now a beautiful and mysterious chapel, it was once a hole in the earth, filled with filthy straw, into which the Son of God was cast after being beaten and assaulted.

Like other prisoners Christ waited in this living tomb before being led to a fate worse than being buried alive. It was the end of him and of his teaching, and the religion of salvation he had proclaimed. It was oblivion; his followers were filled with dread. We have seen from the account of the agony in the garden that he himself was filled with dread. Christian tradition believes that at least symbolically he took on himself all the dread of every child of God who ever lived.

It was the dread of nothingness, emptiness, and ultimate failure that Christ accepted that night. "My Father, if this cannot pass unless I drink it, thy will be done" (Mt 26:42). Every mature human being must face the possibility of dread. It must come sooner or later. When it does, we should recall several things.

1. Try to share your dread with another. Sharing dread is far better than facing it alone. However, we often must bear it alone because others will shy away from our dread. We may have done this ourselves. Haven't you ever felt that you failed to visit a dying friend simply because you were afraid of the other person's dread? A person in dread needs to find someone to share it with.

2. Remember that dread can be useful. It pushes us to the ultimate. In fact, dread gives us a chance to experience and pursue hope. Dread puts all of life in a valid perspective for the believer. It presents us with ultimate issues like those which Moses put before the children of Israel: "Choose life, choose death, choose a blessing, choose a curse."

   Some of us have lived through situations of dread and terror. Later we were able to pick up the pieces and move on. How did we do it? The answer is in our next consideration.

3. Let dread bring you to a living trust and vibrant faith in God. Dread evokes from the depths of our being a powerful human response. I must go on. And yet there is no way to go on, so I will cling to my salvation. I will call out to Christ as St. Peter did on the sea of Galilee, "Lord, save me, I am perishing."

Dread can be very useful for individuals and society. Who would be so interested in peace if the specter of nuclear war was not so terrible? When people thought of war in earlier times they imagined colorful uniforms, knights in armor, the pulsing of the kettledrum and the call of the trumpet. Now there is nothing to think of but fire and ashes. And how many have turned to God because of a dread of hell? One has to be thankful to God that human beings are equipped with a sense of dread. It can drive us to sanity and even propel us into the arms of our Savior.

Fear

We now turn our attention to fear, a much more common emotion than dread. Fear is the apprehension that what we cherish is about to be lost. Unlike dread, fear comes in many degrees. We can be a little fearful but not a little dreadful. We fear a parking ticket, an embarrassment, missing a plane. We fear sickness and the effects of old age. We fear the future and we often live with fears from the past. We fear so much and so often that psychologists from St. Augustine to Freud have seen fear as a universal, underlying experience of life. Freud called it *angst* or basic anxiety.

We all have our pet fears. They are often constant throughout life. They usually begin in childhood and should be clearly recognized by every mature adult.

Let us look at our most common fears which tend to be pervasive and last throughout life.

♦ Fear of being hurt
♦ Fear of illness—sometimes called hypochondria
♦ Fear of rejection by others
♦ Fear of the loss of loved ones
♦ Fear of embarrassment
♦ Fear of being trapped in some situation
♦ Fear of being abandoned or left alone
♦ Fear of being without enough funds
♦ Fear of being controlled by some passion or compulsion
♦ Fear of death

These and many others make up the collection of fears that human beings experience.

It is useful to make a list of our own fears, which will probably include some of the above and some peculiar to us. This helps us recognize how fear can motivate us for good or ill. Sometimes fear makes us wisely cautious and prevents us from rushing in where angels fear to tread. Fear can warn us when we are in real danger. In his notes from *Riders to the Sea,* J. M. Synge quotes an Aran islander as saying, "If a stranger comes here he will be drowned because he is not afraid of the sea. . . . But we who live here are afraid of the sea and we are only drowned now and then."

On the other hand, fear can paralyze us, cause us to hold back, or never begin what we should have started. Think of the immense catalog of things in your own life and in history that have never been done because of fear. Think also of all the evil that has been done because of fear, slavery, the limiting of human rights, or the arms race. Consider societies built on fear, such as Russia or South Africa, and you will see how fear can drive apparently well-meaning people to become monsters. Since fear is so persistent and pervasive, the advice "Know your fears" is worthwhile. Most fears cannot be easily dispelled. They must be worked with and overcome by putting them to good use. If fear and dread are so powerful, they can be directed toward good and can provide motivation for creative work. Fear of illness, for example, has motivated much creative research.

Trust
The way to direct fear is to trust in God. This sounds simplistic, but in fact it is the great message not only of Christianity but of all important world religions. Before we turn again to what the spiritual writers of our own faith say about trust, let us pause and sample what has been written in other religions about the importance of trusting God.

Ramakrishna, a nineteenth century Hindu spiritual writer, taught: "Those who surrender their hearts and souls to God, those who are devoted to Him and have taken refuge in Him, do not worry much about things, about money. As they earn so they spend. The money comes in one way and out another. That is what scripture calls 'accepting what comes'."[12] This advice sounds like part of the Sermon on the Mount, although it is not much like the ethic with which most of us were brought up. A survey of mystical literature would demonstrate that trust in Divine Providence is constantly stressed as it was by this Hindu sage.

Not only does the Old Testament constantly advise us to trust God through historical accounts, prophetic writings and the psalms, but Jewish mystical writers counsel us in the same way. The medieval Jewish mystic Joseph Kinichsi in the book called *Shakel Hakodesh* wrote: "If you have the help of God, the dry wood of the forest will bear you fruit until you say 'enough': but if He who is above is not with you, then even the garden trees will not bring forth fruit."[13]

Can we even cite all the passages in the New Testament that call for trust in God in the face of terrible fear, even in the face of Calvary? The Gospels make it clear that trust does not mean that we shall go through the world easily. In the midst of the vicissitudes and pains of life, however, God will give us what we need to be saved.

Trust sustained our Lord Jesus Christ through his active and demanding apostolate in the face of unbelievable odds, even when he was rejected and betrayed. Trust went with him to Calvary and it was there when he came out of the tomb. I looked through the Gospels for words that would epitomize the Messiah's trust during his passion and death. There are many such quotations. The following from St. John's Gospel sums up our Lord's whole teaching on trust during his own hour of dread and fear. I offer it for your meditation.

The hour has come for the Son of man to be glorified.
Truly, truly, I say to you,
unless a grain of wheat falls into the earth and dies,
it remains alone;

but if it dies, it bears much fruit.
He who loves his life loses it,
and he who hates his life in this world
will keep it for eternal life.
If any one serves me,
he must follow me;
and where I am,
there shall my servant be also;
if any one serves me,
the Father will honor him (Jn 12:23–26).

The trust of Christ during his life and passion set the tone for the long periods of persecution endured by his disciples and followers for three hundred years. Through the centuries the trust of the young man with the divine vision who saw his work crumbling and his life destroyed by evil men on Good Friday has added to his prayer a realism and power that nothing but his own cross could do. "Thy will be done" is the very foundation of Christian trust.

St. Paul echoed the trust of his Lord and Master in many lines of his Epistles and in his own life. If one were to look for a quotation to sum up all St. Paul wrote about trust, many would choose the following:

Who shall separate us from the love of Christ? Shall tribulation, or distress, or persecution, or famine, or nakedness, or peril, or sword? As it is written, "For thy sake we are being killed all the day long; we are regarded as sheep to be slaughtered." No, in all these things we are more than conquerors through him who loved us. For I am sure that neither death, nor life, nor angels, nor principalities, nor things present, nor things to come, nor powers, nor height, nor depth, nor anything else in all creation, will be able to separate us from the love of God in Christ Jesus our Lord (Rom 8:35–39).

Throughout the history of Christian spirituality the constant advice of the spiritual leaders has been to "cast one's care upon the Lord." It is difficult to select even some of the best writings on this subject. One saint has echoed another. The holy bishop of Geneva, St. Francis de Sales, writing to the first Visitation nuns, cited the example of his own patron, Francis of Assisi.

> St. Francis, sending his children into the fields on a journey, gave them instead of money for their whole provision this advice: Cast your care on our Lord and He will feed you. I say the same to you, my very dear daughters, cast all your heart, your desires, your cares, and your affections on the paternal bosom of God, and He will lead you and carry you where His love wishes you to be.[14]

This letter exemplifies not only the public preaching of St. Francis de Sales but also his personal philosophy which he shared with the little congregation he had founded.

We have similar insights into the personal philosophy of another spiritual writer, St. John of the Cross. A devout woman had written to the saint in her desperation. He hastened to assure her of his care and called her to real confidence in God. We seldom get so clear an insight into the personal kindness and care of this austere man.

> It greatly vexes me to think you believe what you say: this would be very bad after so many kindnesses on your part when I least deserved them. That's all I need now is to forget you! Look, how could this be so in the case of one who is in my soul as you are?

> Since you walk in these darknesses and voids of spiritual poverty, you think that everyone and everything is

failing you. It is no wonder that in this it also seems that God is failing you. But nothing is failing you. . . . He who desires nothing else than God walks not in darkness, however poor and dark he is in his own sight. . . . You are making good progress. Do not worry, but rejoice! Who are you that you should guide yourself? Wouldn't that end up fine!

You were never better off than now, because you were never so humble nor so submissive, nor considered yourself and all wordly things to be so small, nor did you know that you were so evil . . . nor did you follow after the imperfections of your own will and interests as perhaps you were accustomed to do. What is it you desire? What kind of life or method of procedure do you paint for yourself in this life? What do you think serving God involves other than avoiding evil, keeping His commandments, and being occupied with the things of God as best we can? . . .

Rejoice and trust in God, for He has given you signs that you can very well do so, and in fact you must do so. . . . Desire no other path than this and adjust your soul to it for it is a good one. . . . Go to confession when you have something definite; you don't have to discuss these things with anyone. Should you have some problem, write to me about it. Write soon and more frequently.[15]

The simplicity of the road of confidence in God is almost frightening to us. We are so complicated that we believe the secret of leading a good Christian life must be complicated too. But it is as simple as the Gospel—and just as hard to follow.

One of the masterpieces of the spiritual life is a little book that remained unpublished for over a hundred years.

It is called *Abandonment to Divine Providence*. The author, Jean-Pierre de Caussade, was an eighteenth century French Jesuit, spiritual writer and teacher. If you are ready for his teaching you may find this sample helpful.

> The great and solid foundation of the spiritual life is to give oneself to God in order to be the subject of His good pleasure in everything internal and external, and afterwards to forget oneself so completely that one considers oneself as a thing sold and delivered to the purchaser to which one has no longer any right in such a way that the good pleasure of God makes all our joy and His happiness, glory and being become our sole good.
>
> This foundation being laid, the soul has nothing to do save to pass all her life in rejoicing that God is good, abandoning herself so completely to His good pleasure that she is equally content to do this or that, or the contrary, at the disposal of God, without reflecting on the use which His good pleasure makes of her.
>
> To abandon oneself! This then is the great duty which remains to be fulfilled after we have acquitted ourselves faithfully of the duties of our state. The perfection with which this duty is accomplished will be the measure of our sanctity. A holy soul is but a soul freely submitted to the Divine will with the help of grace. All that follows this simple acquiescence is the work of God and not of man.[16]

Oddly enough, the person who follows God with such great confidence will accomplish much more than others for the kingdom of God. I have personally heard such effective apostles of our time as Br. Roger of Taizé, Bishop

James Walsh of Maryknoll, Archbishop Helder Camara of Brazil and Mother Teresa of Calcutta all say the same thing. Acceptance of the creative will of God, and effectively doing what we perceive to be that will with courage and indifference to personal obstacles, is the secret of real success in the kingdom. In the face of unspeakable obstacles this faithful confidence in God has achieved and will continue to accomplish all lasting good for the reign of God in human hearts.

Two Cells
At the end of the last chapter I invited you in spirit to visit the cell of St. Philip Howard, and the torture room where St. Edmund Campion was stretched and broken on the rack. Many good Christians, Catholic and Protestant, including St. Margaret Pole and Lady Jane Grey, lost their lives in that awful prison. They died in a fearsome conflict, hoping they would come to see the imperishable kingdom. They exemplify the practice of trust in God in the most difficult circumstances of fear and dread.

A few hours' drive from the Tower of London, in the gentle meadows of East Anglia, is another kind of cell in the town of Norwich. Attached to the church of St. Julian, recently rebuilt on an ancient site, is the reconstituted cell of a fourteenth century anchoress, known to us only by her title, the blessed Lady of St. Julian. Her mystical revelations and commentaries on these are among the most insightful and moving writings of the English mystics. The quiet beauty of the cell and of the adjacent church accidentally gives the impression that Julian lived her life in quiet tranquillity. Nothing could have been further from the truth. She was one of the first pastoral counselors, spending a good deal of time consoling people at the window of the anchorhold.

She lived her prayerful life of intercession and counsel during the Black Death when a third of Europe's population died. She lived through tyranny and the Peasants' Revolt and the fierce reprisals that followed it. Her original revelations of God's love were written when she lay near death in early life. Her doctrine of perfect trust is symbolized by the vision of a crucifix bursting into bloom—a sign that pain and suffering may be the source of beauty and bear abundant fruit. The following quotations of Dame Julian's are taken from a little book edited by Father Robert Llewellyn, a retired Anglican missionary who has dedicated his life to making her known. They provide an apt meditation for the close of this chapter.[17]

He Holds Us When We Fall

A mother may sometimes let her child fall and suffer in various ways so that it may learn by its mistakes. But she will never allow any real harm to come to the child because of her love. And though earthly mothers may not be able to prevent their children from dying, our heavenly mother Jesus will never let us, his children, see death. For he is all might, all wisdom and all love. Blessed may he be!

When we fall he holds us lovingly, and graciously and swiftly raises us. In all this work he takes the part of a kind nurse who has no other care but the welfare of her child. It is his responsibility to save us, it is his glory to do it, and it is his will we should know it.

Utterly at home, he lives in us for ever.

We Shall Not Be Overcome

Though we are in such pain, trouble and distress, that it seems to us that we are unable to think of anything except how we are and what we feel, yet as soon as we may, we are to pass lightly over it, and count it as nothing. And why? Because God wills that we should understand that if we know him and love him and reverently fear him, we shall have rest and be at peace. And we shall rejoice in all that he does.

I understood truly that our soul may never find rest in things below, but when it looks through all created things to find its self, it must never remain gazing on its self, but feast on the sight of God its maker who lives within.

He did not say, "You shall not be tempest-tossed, you shall not be work-weary, you shall not be discomforted." But he said, "You shall not be overcome." God wants us to heed these words so that we shall always be strong in trust, both in sorrow and in joy.

Chapter IV

Envy, Animosity and Forgiveness

Envy

The phenomenon of envy is constantly observed in Scripture, from Genesis to Revelation. It did untold damage in Eden, and later to Cain and Abel. Envy showed itself in the house of Abraham, in the testing of the Israelites at the time of Moses, and it destroyed King Saul. David, Isaiah and Jeremiah all suffered because of envy. In David's case his own envy was often to blame; in the case of the prophets, it was the envy of others. Our Lord was the object of murderous envy. Even today prophets and saints feel the sting of envy, and this condition will continue until the end of the world.

Envy is a particular form of resentment which arises from the desire to possess what another person appears to possess. Because we experience envy long before the use of reason—when we are in the nursery or the playpen with our brothers and sisters—this attitude has a great infantile irrationality about it. There is nothing logical about envy, and, at times, nothing voluntary. It is one of those peculiar emotional states which can come over a person when least expected or desired. Psychology would suggest that this irresistible power and irrationality is explained precisely because it begins so early in life.

It is not wise or realistic to hope to be rid of all feelings of envy in this life. To be completely free of them would be comparable to being without any feelings of fear or anger. This would be an angelic state, which cannot be a human goal.

No, the struggle with this feeling must be realistic. Understanding our own envy can teach us a great deal about ourselves. I don't mind revealing that the struggle with my own envy has taught me much about myself.

One has first to recognize the presence of envy, whether it be in oneself or demonstrated by someone else. Both circumstances are always embarrassing. It is embarrassing to admit that one has given in to such a childish vice, and oddly enough it is also embarrassing to admit that someone else is envious of us. I am not sure why, but when I perceive envy directed toward me, I pretend that it is not there. Even though this denial may appear to be an act of charity or forgiveness on my part, it is ultimately a denial of reality. A little white lie told to oneself never solves problems. Truth is the acceptance of reality, and it is the truth about envy as well as about other things, that makes us free.

Having admitted that envy is present, we must then determine if we are envious or someone is envious of us, or both. Frequently envy is found on both sides. It is like a weed which can grow in a beautiful garden. People who love each other deeply can be jealous of each other. Very good people can find envy lurking in their own hearts, and are often jealous in spite of themselves. If brothers and sisters can be envious and husbands and wives can be jealous of each other, then we should not be surprised to find envy among our friends. Don't be afraid to look at your own envy, or at someone else's envy of you. While it is not always helpful to point out another's envy, it is certainly valuable to notice it in oneself and to identify it clearly when it is directed toward oneself.

Psychologists say that the beginning of envy or jealousy is sibling rivalry. This is the clash of egocentric needs between children, and even between infants. Since young children have no ability to perceive or relate to other people's needs, their own desires are of paramount importance. The fulfillment of these needs is the young child's only goal in life. The needs of others are not perceived.

Parents and parent surrogates are the source of need fulfillment and so children easily clash, vie with each other, and sometimes experience hatred toward a rival for parental attention. Parents who carefully handle the introduction of a new-born child into the family constellation, and who try to balance their affection and responses to their children, will avoid serious mishaps with sibling rivalry. The parents' worst mistake is to show favoritism because children cannot make subtle distinctions. A child who perceives that he is not the favorite may interpret this as total rejection. Honest parents know that for unknown reasons they tend to favor a particular child. Unless they deal wisely with this, they do that child no favors and accidentally cause grief and envy in their other children.

So much for the psychological origins of envy. It is also one of the roots of original sin. We see it in the relationship between Adam and Eve, and it is clearly spelled out in the story of Cain and Abel. Even though we are created to love God and our neighbor as ourselves, envy can enter our lives easily and impede the basic requirement of Christian love. It is our spiritual enemy from the beginning.

We know little about the world that preceded our own universe. Our meager knowledge suggests that envy played a large role in the fall of the angels. Scripture makes it clear that we have a spiritual adversary whom we call the devil or Satan. His motivation for "wandering through the world seeking the ruin of souls" is nothing more than envy. He has certainly affected many lives with envy and resentment. What vice gripped the heart of Judas, or that of the high priests? Envy was instrumental in the fall of the angels and in the fall of man and in the crucifixion.

Envy is not only a constant source of pain to its victims, but it is also a persistent and dangerous source of sin. It is a wound in human nature which is likely to become infected. It is an open invitation to evil, even in the hearts of the good. The obvious conclusion is that we must be constantly on guard against envy—not so much against its presence which is unavoidable, but against its spreading and deeply disrupting our relationships and our spiritual life. Envy always impedes the work that God seeks to do within us.

Animosity

Envy, or jealousy (I use the terms interchangeably), opens the door to animosity. This term expresses something less than hatred but more than annoyance. Animosity means that a person's mind is turned against someone else. Unlike anger or annoyance which can be temporary and passing, animosity is a more permanent state. It collects things that can be used against others. Everything done by others is seen in a bad light. Many good people have a tendency to preserve past injustices, saving them as the ancient Egyptians saved vials of tears to remind themselves of past griefs. Combine injustice collecting together with envy and you will surely get animosity.

Like envy, animosity can co-exist with love. Complicated people can love and hate the same person at the same time for almost the same reasons. I have occasionally spoken to people who lived with someone whom others considered a saint. These people often had both positive and negative feelings toward the holy person, and often for the same reasons. For example, the potential saint was a person of great prayer—too great, in fact. Or the saint had great humility—which was too great to live with. I recall a very saintly friar who always showed up when things were not quite up to the mark. Someone was chatting away during the great silence or having a soda during prayer time. This unfortunate habit of appearing at the wrong time won this dear old soul the title of "Creeping Moses."

Some scholars believe that the mysterious psychological process underlying the betrayal of Judas and the failure of all the apostles was precisely this same kind of animosity toward the Master they loved. It seems at least plausible that his humility and unwillingness to use his mysterious powers against his critics may have caused a resentment they all shared but were unwilling to record.

Of course, animosity is directed not only at saints. We feel animosity toward friends for being demanding or for slighting us, toward colleagues for being competitive, and toward enemies for not accepting and agreeing with us. If you are a complicated neurotic, you may even resent people who like you just because they like you and make you feel guilty because they overestimate your virtues. The weeds of resentment and animosity can grow in any soil.

What should we do when we recognize our own animosity, that permanent negative feeling toward someone else, perhaps even someone we love?

First, we must look at the roots of the animosity. What dark side of our being has been stirred up? It is usually our childish self-centeredness. All of us really want to be at center stage, and we resent it when that position is occupied even by someone we love. How deep are the wounds of sin? How dangerous these words are to those who deny them, and to those who cover up tendencies to sin with a smile or false benignity. A wound ignored and denied is much more likely to infect.

Another sort of animosity is the feeling that we are being dominated, not allowed to be what we would like to be. While it is true that everyone is called to be his or her best self and only God knows that best self, it is also true that a person needs human encouragement and guidance to grow. Instead of accepting encouragement and the fruits of another person's experience, we often balk like little children who are told not to play in a busy street. What our animosity is actually revealing is a certain perversity in human nature which says, "I will not serve."

Animosity can also reveal the need to be the center of another person's affection in a disproportionate way. In marriage and family life, animosity arises at times because of someone's egocentric need to possess another completely, and the other person cannot or will not comply. The desire to possess completely ought to be directed only at God, who is the sole source of our perfect fulfillment. Such absolute expectations for another's affection give rise to unreasonable emotional demands and lead to resentment and manipulation. In every marriage there is a need for some independence.

Forgiveness
What do we do with envy and animosity? My answer is to show forgiveness. That may surprise you. You probably thought that the answer would simply be "charity," described so beautifully by St. Paul in 1 Corinthians 13 as "patient and kind . . . rejoicing at the truth . . . enduring all things. . . . " Is charity not the opposite of envy and animosity? Of course it is, but if one has been very infected by envy and resentment, it is too late simply to come along and paint a coat of charity over the whole thing. That could be simply a veneer. St. Paul's picture of Christian charity is a goal which we reach after a journey. The first step on the journey is forgiveness that goes deep within oneself. We must forgive before the other person requests it or does something to deserve our forgiveness. If envy is present, we

must start with forgiveness. It is the beginning of charity if envy is present. True charity has its source in God. It is his gift. Before we can receive the gift we must prepare for it by forgiveness.

Forgiveness of Self

First we must forgive ourselves because we are always conflicted by our own envy and animosity. Even in the midst of our rage and fury, something within tells us how wrong it all is. To forgive ourselves we need to believe that we are forgiven by God. We must meditate on God's forgiveness of us. Even if you have to struggle to believe it, even if there are voices of guilt and shame screaming inside you, believe in the depths of your soul that you have been forgiven.

I must struggle with self-forgiveness. As a priest I dispense the mysteries of God's love. I have always believed that God and his Son loved us all, even in our sins. I constantly tell people that they are forgiven. I love to hear confessions and celebrate the sacrament of reconciliation. Next to offering the Eucharist it is the most meaningful thing I do. I believe that people are forgiven. I even believe that I am forgiven, but I have come to realize that I did not accept this completely. Yes, I believe that I am forgiven enough to be saved if I die. I underwent dangerous open heart surgery in 1983 and I believed that I would be saved if I did not wake up after the operation. Yet I did not have a deeply felt, emotionally strong belief that God loved me. I am ashamed to admit this, because God has given me so many graces. Somehow I just could not accept it all. I am comfortable in the role of a miserable sinner, even though I have tried to live the Christian life since I was a child. Every day since First Communion has brought new evidence of my complete failure to be a disciple. Yet I believe that God forgives and loves me.

I believed, but I did not know from experience that God loved me. And for this reason I could continue to nourish and cherish resentments. I could collect injustices, secretly cry over my wounds, and cultivate my garden of envy. Yet the realization grew that Christ loved me.

Gradually I became more aware of Christ's love not only for me, but for others too. He loves those whom I love. He loves my enemy because he loves me and we were both Christ's enemy. We have both participated in the great tidal wave of evil that washed around him at the cross. He loves all of us: me, my enemy, my friend who I think has let me down, and all the people I think have hurt me. I can forgive them because I can forgive myself.

I pray that you may have come to this realization already. Don't wait too long. You must believe that you are forgiven. The following quotation is one of many that speaks of our forgiveness by God. It is strange. This has always been one of my favorite passages, and yet I have come to read it in a totally new light.

We know that in everything God works for good with those who love him, who are called according to his purpose. For those whom he foreknew he also predestined to be conformed to the image of his Son, in order that he might be the first-born among many brethren. And those whom he predestined he also called; and those whom he called he also justified; and those whom he justified he also glorified.

What then shall we say to this? If God is for us, who is against us? He who did not spare his own Son but gave him up for us all, will he not also give us all things with him? Who shall bring any charge against God's elect? It is God who justifies;

who is to condemn? Is it Christ Jesus, who died,
yes, who was raised from the dead, who is at the
right hand of God, who indeed intercedes for us? (Rom 8:28–
   34).

But suppose you say to yourself, "I don't feel forgiven." Believe it anyway! Many times we have to believe
things when we don't feel them, even though they are true.
If you can believe that you are forgiven, that God has first
loved you, then you can move on to forgiving yourself for
the effects of original sin, for actual sins, for your bad habits
and mistakes, and for your animosity and envy. You can
begin to see yourself as a child of God. You find yourself in
his arms in the unqualified unconditional love that each
one of us has been looking for from others. Slowly strength
will come to you.

Forgiveness of Others

Having realized God's forgiveness and having forgiven
yourself, you are prepared to deal with your envy. You no
longer feel like an outcast who has been rejected by God.
There is no longer a sense of having been cheated by life,
your family, even by God himself. A person who feels
cheated, deprived and put upon is bound to feel envious.
You cannot expect anything but envy and animosity from
someone whose world has crashed around him and who
lives on nothing but shame and fear.

Only a few years ago I would have dismissed all this as
pious platitudes. Of course I believed that Christ loved me
and everybody else. I trusted him to lead me to salvation,
but I did not realize that he loves us. He does.

I did not yet see the precious blood of Jesus Christ
descending over the world like a great tidal wave of forgiveness and salvation. I am aware that not everyone will

believe and accept that they are loved and forgiven. Unfortunately not all of us are going to overcome envy and animosity because we can feel the power of the precious blood of Jesus in our lives. But it does mean that God's love is there for you and me, even when we neglect it, forget it, and don't accept it.

This awareness has caused me to meditate on Judas, of all people. One Easter Sunday a group of pilgrims and I stood by the Mount of the Ascension and looked over the field of blood, Haceldema. I shuddered when I saw it. I thought of the thirty pieces of silver. Just imagine what glorious page in Church history would have been written if Judas had gone to Calvary instead of hanging himself, if he knelt at the foot of the cross and asked forgiveness. His bitter regret would have changed to contrition and sorrow. His wrath at God and Christ and self would have been turned into forgiveness. The blood which he had caused to be shed would have first descended on him to wash away his sins. Was it possible? Of course. Judas could have been the greatest apostle of all, but he turned away from forgiveness. There might be a shrine today at Haceldema, known as the Church of St. Judas the Apostle. Alas, it never came to be. We need desperately to believe in our own forgiveness. We need to accept it and share it with others. We need to accept the fact that God, in Christ, loves, forgives and cherishes us. Then we can gradually forgive others and overcome our envy and animosity.

Frequently in popular psychological writing certain ideas are presented for the reader's consideration. They are usually general and abstract concepts, almost always unproven and unprovable, but apparently helpful from the author's viewpoint. They range from telling yourself that you're "O.K.," to becoming convinced that we have to trust others or be more assertive. My suggestion is that you begin with the idea of forgiveness. Start to believe deeply that you are forgiven. Unlike convincing yourself that you should be more assertive, believing that you are really forgiven and loved by God will require the help of the Holy Spirit.

Coming to the realization that God and his Son love you, your friends, and even your enemies will require a good deal of time and grace. But it will gradually heal the wound of envy and animosity that festers in most of us.

Envy is overcome by forgiveness and love, but it is never an easy accomplishment. I looked for a story to illustrate the power of forgiveness and love to overcome envy and bitter reactions to it. My memory brought me back to an ancient monastery in the port city of Genoa. I was standing in a cloister corridor with Padre Rudolfo, whose tattered habit and ascetic face were highlighted by a shaft of sunlight falling into the darkness. He recounted a story of envy on the part of a former superior which had inflicted deep pain on an old man. But the old friar's forgiveness and charity had overcome all obstacles.

Il Santo Padre

The old brother was preparing for a busy day by his customary prayers and devotions in the baroque chapel of the monastery. He had already set up his equipment for the day's work. His brown cloak lay over the choir stall behind him. He had arranged a collection of bags and cans with which he begged food for the friars. Everyone knew that in fact he gave away more food than he received. Wearing grotesque, heavy sandals, he tramped up and down the side alleys of the busy port of nineteenth century Genoa. He smiled as he thought of the poor children of the port who grew up on the docks where they would eventually work all their lives. They would be waiting for him, and he was so pleased today because a kind lady had sent him a hundred beautiful holy cards of the Bambino Gesù. Even the tough ones would forget their assumed anticlericalism and cynicism and line up for their little card.

He would have to talk to some of them very directly. There was a rumor that one fellow was hitting his wife when he was drunk. And the others on Dock 5 were good boys, but they kept calling him "Santo Padre." He was neither holy nor a priest, he thought, but simply a little brother. Oh, he must not forget, he promised a cigar to old Carlo. He had taken one from the common recreation room but did not smoke it, out of respect for the Madonna. He would give it to Carlo. He hoped that the superior had not noticed him slip it up his sleeve.

As Brother Francesco Maria came out of the chapel he was startled to see the Father Guardian waiting for him. The superior looked very stern, as always, but this morning he looked annoyed as well.

He spoke to the brother in an icy tone. "You know, Francesco, you are not the only saint in Genoa. There are other saints who are not so much in the public eye. Some of them live quietly in this friary. You stay home for a while, and I will send others out to do the begging. They will not distribute our alms to everybody who gives them a story."

Francesco was crushed. He smiled—almost a reflex action—and went back into the chapel. What about the poor, the sailors, the children? What about Carlo? They would all be looking for him. Would they think he forgot them? His heart was broken. But he never complained. He never held a grudge. He went over to the crucifix. In spite of himself and his old age, the tears of bitterness ran down his long beard. "I never said I was a saint. I never acted like a saint, God knows. The Guardian must have heard about those boys calling me 'the holy father.' I can do nothing now but pray for all my friends."

Some months later, cholera struck Genoa, as it often did. Hundreds died every day. Francesco wanted to do something but he was not permitted to go out. He prayed late into the night for the victims. He listened for each scrap of news about who had died on the docks. "Sophia and her little Maria, that little angel, had died and were already in the common grave set up by the city."

Late one night when Brother Francesco left the chapel, he came upon the Father Guardian checking the doors. Almost on an impulse as a result of his prayer, Francesco stopped the superior. "Please, Padre, may I ask a permission." "What is it now, Francesco?" came the cold reply. "May I have your permission," the brother asked, "to offer my poor life as a prayer to the Lord so that the cholera will stop?" The Guardian was not impressed with such theology. He was annoyed more than he meant to be. But this man irritated him so much even though he recognized his simplicity. This silly old brother caused him to commit so many sins of unkindness which he was always confessing. Consequently his answer was unnecessarily sharp. "I don't care what you do," the Guardian said. Francesco went back to the chapel.

They woke the Superior when it was almost dawn. Francesco had cholera. It could not be, the priest thought. He had seen him a few hours before. When the Superior got to the room Brother Francesco was almost gone. God had received his sacrifice. Astonished, the Superior told the other friars what had happened the night before. The word spread through Genoa like wildfire, because Brother Francesco Maria of Comporosso was the last person to die of cholera in Genoa. His body was the last to be buried without a funeral because of the fear of contagion. Francesco

Maria Croese of Comporosso is now buried in the friary chapel because he was canonized a saint. Padre Rudolfo who told me this story was the postulator of his cause.

When I asked a man in Genoa station to direct me to the Capuchin Friary, he smiled and said, "Oh, the 'Holy Father' is just down the street." The "Holy Father" of Genoa had been dead since 1866. He was not only a victim of cholera. He was more the victim of the envy of another basically good man. But his love and forgiveness had been victorious. Forgiveness went first; then charity could do its marvelous work.

Chapter V

Selfishness, Self-Love and Charity

I used to think it was easy to get over selfishness and self-love. My parents went to great lengths to teach their children to be generous, to do things for one another and for other people. I thought it was easy. There were many old people living in our neighborhood and my mother was forever sending one of them a piece of cake or a jar of homemade jelly. We always felt good when we returned from these errands, usually rewarded with candy. I enjoyed interrupting my playtime to go on these errands. I thought I had learned to overcome selfishness. I wish now it was that easy.

We are all born with a powerful drive to fulfill our own needs. A child without this drive will perish. A child who never gets beyond this drive will be pathologically immature. Only when this drive is curbed and shaped do we begin to deal with self-preservation in a way moderated by the needs of others and give up being absolutely self-centered. You may remember when you stopped fighting to be the first in line in second grade, or when you took time to help another student in need in high school. This struggle to open your heart to compassion had probably begun because of the good example of family members or of teachers and friends.

But there are teachers who also helped us to learn about our selfishness in a reflex way. These are the selfish. I remember them well. I think I met them for the first time when I was a caddy on a golf course. There were people who were demanding, discourteous and ungrateful. Sometimes they inspired pity, but more often they caused a flash of anger or disgust. Many of the caddies were thinking of being priests. We thought we were different from some of our clients. Though these people had money, they often lacked the basic values we had learned from our hard-working, dedicated parents.

I lived with this illusion of unselfishness for a long time. Then one day I was pulled up short. Someone accused me of being selfish. I was one of the generous ones, the courteous kindly people. I was selfish! I remember times when, in anger or disappointment, people pointed out my selfishness to me. These were among the most painful encounters I experienced in my life. What about the jars of jelly my mother made and I delivered? Was it all in vain? Was I not generous and giving? What were they talking about?

I recall one very painful incident when I was a young priest. I was rushing to give a talk at a college and was almost late. When I got near the Throggs Neck Bridge in the Bronx there was a line a half mile long. I spotted some outdoor phone booths by the side of the highway. After some difficulty, I reached one and dialed the college switchboard. A mechanical voice said, "Eighty cents, please." Thank heaven I had ninety cents in change. I quickly put in the correct amount and listened to the loudest silence I had ever heard. Nothing! I went to another phone booth and called the operator, explaining that I had just lost my eighty cents and asked her to place the call. She said she could not but would arrange to send me a check for eighty cents. I pleaded with her, pointing out that the switchboard would not accept a collect call—all to no avail. Then I got on my high horse and told her that I was not lying. I was a clergyman. Then, with a sweet southern accent, she answered, "Well, if you are a reverend you ought to be more polite." I stood there looking at the phone as if I had just heard the trumpet of the last judgment. I felt guilty and ashamed. My selfishness had been recognized by a fellow member of Christ's faithful.

As I waited for the toll gate to come into sight, I asked myself the following questions: Could there be selfishness and self-seeking tendencies in my attempts to be generous? Could I be giving with strings attached, with hidden agendas, with subtle expectations? Was I working for the Gospel or for myself? After thirty years of religious life, was I still selfish?

And, of course, the answer was yes. The leftovers of childhood are deeply embedded in us and can be relinquished only when we perceive that they are no longer necessary for our survival. The human psyche does not give up the defenses of the past until we believe that we no longer need them. The saddest thing about self-centered and selfish adults is that they really believe they need to be that way.

Let's take a look at these distinctions between selfishness and self-love. Our goal will be to overcome them by God's gift of charity.

Selfishness

Selfishness, unlike self-love, is always a vice. It may be defined as regressive behavior in which an individual reverts to an immature way of acting. It is the reappearance of the self-centeredness of early childhood at a later age when this is no longer appropriate. What was a necessary inclination in a child, causing him to put himself first and impetuously seek his own needs, is a vice in an older person. This fact is so much a part of the common understanding of human behavior and interpersonal relationships that extraordinary selfishness is recognized in psychotherapy as a serious personality disorder.

Unfortunately there are certain situations in which there is likely to be regression into profound selfishness. We may all confront such situations at one time or another.

1. Sickness: A person who is physically or mentally unwell for a long period of time is likely to become very self-centered and demanding. Ask a nurse!

2. Prolonged periods of emotional or physical stress may cause a person to become frantically self-centered.

3. A situation in which someone is deprived of emotional support may cause a reaction of self-centeredness and apparent selfishness. For instance, a neglected husband or wife may appear to become selfish. Actually, the spouse may have been trying to be generous and the efforts were ignored. Selflessness breeds selfishness in others.

4. Periods of psychological life-stress may cause a person to become rather selfish. A genuinely kind and generous person going through mid-life crisis may suddenly become uncharacteristically self-centered.

These common situations of stress should make us stop and ask: Are we getting selfish ourselves? Did we ever really get over our childhood self-centeredness successfully? Have we left childhood behind for good? The answer is no. The potential for regression to selfishness is always there.

This tendency toward regression is probably the psychological foundation of the seven capital sins, or at least of covetousness, gluttony and sloth.

Even though the tendency to selfishness is deeply ingrained in us, there are ways to combat it. For example, you ought to recognize and honestly appraise the limits of your ability to cope with stress and extra demands. When you find that you are feeling testy, easily annoyed or stingy because you are overburdened, it is time to take stock. You may be a little unrealistic about what you can take on.

Frequently, generous people are taken advantage of. This is usually not done through malice, but because other people are desperate. We have to protect ourselves sometimes in order to recoup energies. It is of little use to remember that a saint would not complain under such circumstances. We are not saints, so we must have the humility to admit our limitations.

Some people may try to exceed these limitations. They may go the last mile and be generous even to taxing their inner resources to the breaking point. If you decide to do this, remember that you have chosen to do it and it is going to be tough. We will say more about this when we come to charity.

Self-Love

We can now look at the mysterious tendency called self-love, as distinct from selfishness. Self-love is one of the most perplexing phenomena in psychology, especially since it is often the other side of an equally intense self-hate. Self-love is a term used to describe many attitudes. It can mean simply the childish tendency to put oneself first, which we have just discussed. It may also mean that dark reality when childish selfishness begins to crystallize as a permanent component of an adult personality. It can become a demon that devours a person's good qualities, so that he or she slips into the idolatry of self. Self-love as a vice is no respecter of persons. It can touch the prelate and the peddler, the great and the small. It can masquerade as victim or prophetic spirit.

It can be self-indulgent or self-righteous, or both. This kind of self-love is so dangerous that our Lord made the denial of it a prerequisite for the apostolate. "If anyone will come after me, he must deny himself and take up his cross and follow me." We must always strive against self-love of the kind I have described.

We all live with traces of this self-love. It is like a bodily infection. We all have bacteria in our system to promote the digestion of food, yet these must be controlled or we will die. So it is with self-love. It requires a constant effort to keep the infection of self-love under control.

But what about legitimate self-love? Is there such a thing? I used to think not. Occasionally I have met rather simple people with uncomplicated needs who simply accept themselves. They neither admire nor reject themselves. If they avoid the danger of complacency they can have a gentle self-acceptance which is legitimate self-love. Like many other people, I have struggled all my life with self-hate, with a rejection of self that was neurotic and dangerous. Unfortunately this self-hate is not humility. (I have rarely been accused of humility.) I had somehow come to believe that I could do nothing well. I was and still am frightened of my critics, and I fear my friends may desert me, if they discover who I really am. There emerges a strange hybrid indeed: self-hate and self-love together.

Self-love when joined to self-hate becomes a desperate need to prove oneself, to love oneself, to be rid of the fear that no one else really loves you. If it gets out of hand, such a sentiment may block human relationships and ultimately lead to profound loneliness and depression. This strange mixture of self-love and self-hate, known as narcissism, may cause a compulsive striving to get ahead. It constantly complains that no one cares. It can lead to bitterness, negativism, and self-deceit. What is the antidote to all this madness? What, you ask, can be done to keep the selfishness of childhood at bay and to cope with the tendencies toward self-hate and self-love?

Charity

The answer, I believe, is to be found in a mysterious, and often misused, word: charity. Let us skip over all the definitions of charity as philanthropy, or brotherhood, however helpful these may be. Charity is completely a gift of God, which he bestows as a special grace. Although it builds on certain human qualities, it can begin to operate at times without them. Charity helps us first to accept ourselves. This may sound paradoxical, considering all that I have said above, but I suspect it is true.

Are we not to love our neighbor as ourselves? Are we not told to love God because he has first loved us and sent his Son to die for us? If God loves us, and we are to love our neighbor as we love ourselves, there must be charity that is true love of self. Charity means to do good to another, to wish them the best, to seek someone's good. Charity toward self calls us to seek our own highest good, which is God, and to wish to attain it. However, because of the fall of the human race and its consequence, original sin, we need the special gift of God's love to do this in reality. Charity does indeed begin at home, that is, with ourselves.

I don't know about you, but I have a good deal of trouble with the notion of loving self. I don't like it. In fact I get sick at the notion of loving myself. The words recall all the self-centeredness of which I am so ashamed. (If you are feeling sick at the notion, please stick with me, comforted by the knowledge that I don't like it either.)

The overwhelming fact of creation and life is that the incomprehensible force and mind that made all these things loves us. That force and mind we call God. We have

been taught by his Son to call him "Father." We have seen
the immensity and glory of his love, revealed in the incarnation, the passion and the resurrection of Christ. We are
compelled by the good things around us to believe as best
we can that God loves us. You must believe that he loves
you, and I must believe with all my being that he loves me.
And then the deep rivers of love will begin to flow in our
souls. I believe that the gift of charity really unlocks great
rivers deep in our being, which has been created in the
image and likeness of God. But the rivers of love must be
freed. The dam of selfishness must be dislodged, and the
rusty floodgates of self-love must be opened. The rocky sea
walls of self-hate must be pierced. And this can be done
only by God's grace. It is the Holy Spirit's work to make us
come alive in the image of Christ.

If you want to love, you must be willing to be vulnerable. The Gospel makes it clear that if you extend your
hand often enough in a gesture of love, someone will drive
a nail through it. If you love others, you may be deceived,
betrayed and abandoned. If you love Christ, you must walk
the difficult road to Calvary. But you will begin to see yourself borne by powers that are beyond you. It may not be
very noticeable at first. It may be no more than patience
with criticism, or extra generosity after you have done
enough. You may feel firmly drawn to God even when you
can't pray. You will begin to change. And this is the effect
of charity, which will overflow into a love for others that
goes beyond affection or pity.

For most people love is a powerful emotion which
draws us to give the utmost to the one we love. It calls forth
the best, the most profound, the most extreme. Yet if love
is merely an emotion, it cannot last. But love can also mean
dependency, and this can last for a lifetime and cause neg-

ative feelings, so that people who love each other frequently argue and bicker for years.

But even out of emotion and dependency may come dedication and conviction. Here is where the grace of charity can really enter in. Mature love does not waver; it is the strongest force in the world. Love becomes holy when it is touched by God's grace; it is reverent, filled with awe, and utterly undeterred by obstacles. It is inspired so that it often accomplishes much more than is reasonably expected. Love is like great art: it contains more than it appears to, and it says more than it expresses. Charity can effect good things for hundreds of years whether it be for a family, a cause, or a faith. A person who has come to the love of God in this mature sense may or may not feel any great emotion, but there will be faith, as well as total, reverent dedication to God and his children. Consequently, such a person will accomplish things beyond all expectation. Love will leave self-hate and selfishness so far behind that there will be no vestige of either of them at the end of the journey.

Having considered love in its aspects of selfishness and self-love, we can perhaps meditate with some new insight on one of the most familiar quotations in Scripture. We should reread this great passage occasionally. If we are making progress on our journey it should have an ever deeper and richer meaning for us.

> But earnestly desire the higher gifts, and I will show you a still more excellent way.
>
> If I speak in the tongues of men and of angels, but have not love, I am a noisy gong or a clanging cymbal. And if I have prophetic powers, and understand all mysteries and all knowledge, and if I have all faith, so as to remove mountains, but have not love, I am

nothing. If I give away all I have, and if I deliver my body to be burned, but have not love, I gain nothing.

Love is patient and kind; love is not jealous or boastful; it is not arrogant or rude. Love does not insist on its own way; it is not irritable or resentful; it does not rejoice at wrong, but rejoices in the right. Love bears all things, believes all things, hopes all things, endures all things. Love never ends (1 Cor 12:31—13:8).

Love inspired by the virtue of charity is one of the most potent forces in world history. It is perhaps the most powerful force in the world, when one looks at history apart from the superficial events that make up political history. Underneath the apparently great events are those that will have everlasting significance: the holy love of a parent, child, or spouse. These are rarely in books, but they are the real events of history.

Two Women Who Loved Against All Odds

On a visit to New Orleans I tripped over one of the great unknown stories of loving dedication in American church history. It is the story of two women—one black, one white—who loved God and his children more than most of the heroes whose images are in the Capitol in Washington, and who were as dedicated as many people whose statues you will find in churches. During a recent stay at the residence of Archbishop Philip Hannan of New Orleans, two devoted disciples of these women took good care of me. Between them Sister Guadalupe and Sister Aurelia had spent one hundred and four years in religious life. They are members of the Sisters of the Holy Family of New Orleans, the largest order of black sisters in America.[18]

The foundress, Henriette de Lisle, was born in New Orleans in 1813 into a class known as the "free people of color." These were children born to black mothers who had lived—without any of the benefits or protection of marriage—with white men who had come to New Orleans to seek their fortune. Girls born into this class were expected to learn such arts as dressmaking, cooking and dancing from their mothers. They were destined to become, in effect, the common-law wives of French, Spanish, and eventually American men who were unmarried or had left their legal wife far away. In return for this arrangement the people of color were free and could enjoy a fairly affluent life-style. Unfortunately, all the girls were expected to find the right white man, and few of them could marry a boy of their own ethnic group. At the same time New Orleans was filled with white girls and women who could not find someone to marry. It was a sad state of affairs.

Henriette de Lisle believed that she was called to break away from this bondage. She believed that she was called to be a nun, to consecrate her life to God, to free her people from bondage, to care for the neglected black elderly, and to educate the young in religion. In a word, she believed that God had called her to change the world in which she lived. She could join no existing order because of the laws against racial integration. She could not even incorporate her own order of black women as such. Her community was over fifty years old before it had a separate legal status. She founded her community three times before it succeeded. She endured misunderstanding, ridicule, and even threats against her person. But she believed that God's love had called her, and she went on.

While space does not permit me to tell the whole story, one detail of Mother Henriette's life should not go unmentioned. The rendezvous for girls of her social class to meet men who would later become their common-law husbands was known as the Ball Room on Bourbon Street. This building was the very symbol of a genteel bondage. Mother de Lisle eventually bought this building and made it the motherhouse of the Sisters of the Holy Family. She got them right between the eyes!

Astonishing as the works of Mother de Lisle and the first sisters were, especially during the years before the Civil War when the worst oppression of black people took place, there was another equally memorable person in this drama. This is Sister Aliquot, a Frenchwoman who never even got to be a nun canonically. Miss Aliquot and her two sisters came to New Orleans to help with religious education as the severe persecution of the church in France came to an end in 1831. As she came down the gangplank, it gave way and Miss Aliquot fell into the muddy waters of the Mississippi. A young slave jumped in and saved her. It is said that she knelt down on the dock in a puddle of water, and, surrounded by her sisters and the curious onlookers, made a vow to God that she would dedicate her life to the religious education of the black children and slaves. And she did. This was no easy task since it was illegal (and later a capital offense) to teach a slave anything without the permission of his owner.

Because of her vow Miss Aliquot could not join any existing white order, and she was forbidden by law from joining the Sisters of the Holy Family. So she became "Sister" Aliquot on her own, with a close affiliation to the Sisters of the Holy Family. With her habit and her French accent and citizenship she was a rather formidable presence when she called at plantations and asked for permission to teach catechism to the children. I suspect that those who refused were threatened—rightly—with the wrath of God.

Miss Aliquot outlived by one year Mother de Lisle, who died in 1862. By that time the Sisters of the Holy Family were well established but still did not have a legal existence, apart from the Society of the Holy Family which did all kinds of charitable work including education and the care of aged black people. When the Union Army took New Orleans, the soldiers enticed a number of black girls, some of them only ten years old, into the camp for immoral purposes. In the midst of a storm (which she may have actually caused), Sister Aliquot arrived at the camp and intimidated the soldiers so much that all the girls left the camp. A few days later, Sister Aliquot died of pneumonia which she had contracted on the day of the storm.

I do not think that two more remarkable women can be found in the annals of American history. They were victorious because of a charity that goes beyond all obstacles. Along with other black nuns like Mother Theodore Williams, foundress of the Franciscan Handmaids of the Most Pure Heart of Mary in Harlem, they proved that even when everybody misunderstands and despises you, you can do good things if you are motivated by the fire of God's love.

Chapter VI

Self-hate, Hesitancy and Love of God

The bishop sat down at his desk, and, after a time of prayer, thoughtfully began a letter that might be the most important one of his life. Although a man of only forty-seven years, his face looked strained and weary of life. Carefully he framed his words to the Cardinal Prefect of the Congregation for the Propagation of the Faith. After some words of introduction the letter continued:

> I was a little disturbed by the fear that I had done something that so displeased the Holy Father that my resignation would be desirable to him. If this be the case, I am prepared without hesitation to leave the episcopacy. I have taken this burden out of obedience, and I have labored with all my power to fulfill the duties of my office. When the care of temporal things weighed upon my mind, and it seemed to me that my character was little suited to the very cultured world of this city, I made it known to my fellow bishops that it seemed appropriate to me to request my transfer to one or the other see. . . . Indeed, I am much more accustomed to the country, and will be able to care for the people and faithful living in the mountains, in the coal mines and on the farms since I would be among them. I am prepared to resign from the episcopate and to go where I may more securely prepare myself for death and for the account that must be rendered to the Divine Justice.[19]

This letter is totally in keeping with the thought of a man who had the lowest opinion of himself. His personal prayers show the heart of a person who was not only humble but filled with self-hate, which was held in check only by confidence in the love of God. The letter has to be read in light of the fact that in his eight years as bishop he had built dozens of churches, including a cathedral still in use, and founded several religious communities. He really founded the first diocesan educational system in the United States. This man who hated himself so much, and saw himself as such a failure, was St. John Neumann, C.S.S.R., bishop of Philadelphia from 1852 to 1860. His greatest victory was to keep going in spite of his self-hate and to transform it into genuine humility.

Self-Hate
Self-hate can be a most powerful obstacle in the spiritual life, yet it can also be a stepping stone. I am coming more and more to believe that self-hate is the origin of most psychological difficulties. It is at least an essential component of most, if not all, functional mental illness, that is, illness which has no physiological cause. Yet many great people like Bishop Neumann have overcome it by using it to grow in the love of God and neighbor.

Since the term "self-hate" is so shocking, some consideration of its origin will be helpful. A baby must think of himself as the center of the universe. His psychic reality is the center of all he knows. He must love himself and seek his own good and best interests in everything. He is not aware of it but this is a fallen world. Things just don't work the way we want them to. No one, not even a baby, gets exactly what he wants. So the baby gets angry. And if you have seen babies angry and enraged, you know that theirs can be an Olympian wrath, worthy of Jupiter or Thor.

As the child gets older he will at times be disappointed in others and become angry with them and perhaps be punished for his anger. Later he will encounter criticism from his relatives, which may be misdirected by adults or taken in the wrong way by the child. Frequently criticism is motivated not by a desire to be helpful, but by annoyance and pique. A child is likely to see this criticism as the reason for his disappointment in life. He may even come to believe that it is his own fault that he does not get what he wants. He must be doing something wrong. He begins to incorporate this criticism, taking it in and doing things to attract more criticism.

At this point the child has become his own worst enemy. This is the beginning of the serious psychological problem called passive aggression, which becomes a crystalized part of the child's overall adjustment. At best, passive aggression, hatred against self, leads to the self-defeating attitudes that most neurotics cope with. At worst, it can lead to a life of criminal behavior. Passive aggression comes to its ultimate term in suicide, either by a single act or by self-destructive addiction.

The very term self-hate is so shocking that most moderately neurotic people doubt that they suffer from it. Like most of us, however, you feel guilty when you are praised for doing good. You probably anticipate difficulties if the sun shines for three days in a row. I grew up with these feelings, and, at times, even thought they were virtues. Then one day the Lord in his providence decided to use self-hate to help some other people and to resolve some of my own problems.

I was assigned to be chaplain of a large treatment center for disturbed and delinquent boys. I was frightened because I was much less street-wise than the members of my little flock. My friends thought it was hilarious that I should be assigned to work with pre-delinquents and expected me to last only a few weeks. (I stayed fourteen happy years.) I discovered that I could work very easily with these youngsters and could not understand why. Then after a short time I realized that I was struggling with the same thing that was troubling them—self-hate. This was a total surprise to me since I came from a loving home and entered religious life at the earliest possible age. I had never done anything more delinquent than throw an eraser in class (once). My parents were loving and dedicated, but they also tended to be rather critical and were understandably preoccupied with the care of a large family. Like John Neumann, I was not an obvious candidate for the self-hate club. Yet like him I could easily identify with people on the fringe of things—delinquents and very poor people.

If you are wondering whether you have any signs of self-hate, examine the following symptoms of this common psychic wound:

1. Constant disparagement in the appreciation and presentation of self.
2. Lack of care about one's appearance, or, conversely, such great care about one's appearance that it is really an overcompensation.
3. Lack of confidence in one's ability, often overcompensated by compulsive work.
4. Passive-aggressive and self-defeating acts.
5. Preoccupation with death or self-destructive things.
6. A lack of self-respect regarding moral problems by becoming involved with self-demeaning vices.
7. Suicide or thoughts of suicide, which are direct or indirect, namely, alcoholism and other addictions.

You needn't have all of the above to recognize self-hate. Any one or two will do very nicely. Also, it is not necessary to have always been aware of self-hate.

The following letter was written by a young person in the throes of a fierce struggle with self-hate. As often happens, the full weight of repressed self-hate erupted like a volcano at the end of adolescence. In this case, it had precipitated problems with his first adult job and threatened the professional career he had prepared for by obtaining a degree in demanding scientific studies. The occasion of this letter was a visit to his parents on Mother's Day, about eight months after he had begun his new career.

> You seem concerned about how my weekend at home went. There was a good deal of concern as to how I was feeling, if I got enough rest. I suppose it is no secret to many that I have seen my Calvary. I do not understand how those who share my love recognize my very personal pain. I have tried unsuccessfully to conceal it, so now let them see and wonder about me and show a loving concern because they do see a change—bitterly born in pain. Stand by me, please, because you understand. You have been where I am now. This will not be easy or pleasant—or even blessed for either of us. Between us we will accomplish what we have begun. Pray to God that I may some day have the opportunity to be to you what you have been to me.

In another letter the cause of pain was expressed after the young person had returned to work in another state.

> Hello—it's me, the silent suffering young man who has complicated your already complicated life. I feel guilty as hell. I wish I could have really spoken to you when I visited. Through your kind efforts and my hellish state of being you are bearing the brunt of my negative feeling. The persistent buzz of nastiness, of good thoughts turned wicked, prevents me from helping myself. I want you to suffer as little as possible when

you watch me. I want to learn to suffer well and know
that you will be near the phone when I need you.

In this letter self-hate has become very conscious, even
though the person is struggling against it. Self-hate is rarely
as conscious as it is in this letter. When it is, it should be
recognized and talked through, and this is not easy. When
self-hate is unconscious, however, it can do a great deal of
harm, even though it may not be as virulent as when it is
conscious. One of the techniques for overcoming self-hate
is called the healing of memories. This is best done with
another person or with several people who have some
familiarity with the technique. The healing of memories
requires living through the rejection and hate of the past
with all the anger and other experiences of self-hate, and
then surrendering them prayerfully to God. At times we all
need to go through the healing of memories. Informally we
do this in our reveries and memories of the past. But,
unfortunately, instead of healing memories one may at
times simply open old wounds. Prayer for the dead, when
done thoughtfully and carefully, is also a good expression
of the healing of memories.[20]
Self-hate is so powerful and common that many people
have developed their own ways of coping with it. Some of
these ways are likely to lead to further unhappiness, while
others can lead to a productive practice of virtue and
growth in the spiritual life. Self-hate can cause a person to
sink into a self-destructive vice, to set himself up for defeat,
or purposely separate himself from God. If the person turns
to God and asks for help, self-hate may lead to a life of dedicated penance in service of the poor when this gives little
or no reward. If a person recognizes self-hate in his or her
own makeup, it is important to take careful stock of what
is being done with it. Frequently a good Christian who has

self-hate basically under control and uses it to do helpful and creative things may at the same time do little self-destructive things on the side. This is such a familiar picture that I would suggest to the reader who recognizes self-hate to make a serious examination of his or her life-style. If there is behavior that makes no sense, look for signs of self-hate. If self-destructive tendencies are persistent, our comments about practicing the love of God at the end of this chapter will be helpful.

Hesitancy

Self-hate in its less virulent form shows itself as self-disparagement or lack of confidence. I have chosen here to call this hesitancy. It is a hesitancy to do anything good or creative. People will often back away and not use their talents and appear frightened. What is really going on is self-hate in a mild form.

A slogan aimed at overcoming this kind of hesitancy and self-hate has become popular in recent years. It is called "stepping out in faith." This means that a person decides to take a chance with life, facing it in a way that becomes a Christian who believes in the goodness of God.

Hesitancy is quite treacherous. It may appear as prudence, humility, or lack of pride. Indeed, there are situations in which hesitancy is motivated by a self-hate that can mask a peculiar kind of pride. A person who is filled with hesitancy may sit on the sidelines of life and feel that the rest of the world isn't really good enough to know anything about him. Self-hate and hesitancy both lead to a kind of wounded pride. Though it may look like a virtue, hesitancy is not. When all is said and done, the Christian is a believer, that is, someone who seeks to take the kingdom of heaven by storm, a person who runs along the way of God and travels swiftly. St. Paul refers to the Christian as one who runs in such a way as to win the race. Neither hesitancy nor self-hate can be identified as a Christian virtue.

Like self-hate, hesitancy can lead to a virtue if it is overcome and taken beyond its own narrow limits. Just as the self-hating person can turn powerful energies to doing good, so the hesitant person can achieve genuine humility and selflessness. Those trapped in hesitancy are likely to be much less driven and ambitious than victims of self-hate. The energies trapped by hesitancy are gentler and softer. With the help of grace, the hesitant person may develop an honest joy in taking a less conspicuous place in life. He may enjoy being helpful on the sidelines. In religious and parish life one meets many people like this, and if their hesitancy has been transformed by humility they are a joy to know. They can make real spiritual progress because they are willing to do difficult works which receive little recognition. But if the hesitant person's real motive remains a buried self-hate which has never been transcended by the love of God and neighbor, then anger, resentment and eventually self-destructiveness will flare up, causing everyone to wonder what happened.

You may not see any symptoms of self-hate when you look at yourself initially, but watch for signs of hesitancy. It can be a real millstone and impede your progress. Some of the symptoms of hesitancy which spring from self-hate include boredom, fear, criticism of self, lack of belief that we have been called by God to do anything, and cynicism. Ask yourself whether self-hate is present in your life.

The Love of God
The antidote to attitudes built on self-hate is the love of God. Love of God means two things: our love for him and his love for us. Here we are using the second meaning: his love for us. God's love is in fact revealed to us in the

immense conflict with self-hate. When we realize that God loves us it may paradoxically bring our self-hate to a white-hot level of intensity. The realization of God's love can at first be disturbing, humiliating, and cause real guilt. We may be thrown into conflict by realizing that we hate the very person God loves. In the book *The Royal Way of the Cross,* Archbishop Fénelon writes a most revealing passage about the spiritual experience of a person who comes close to God.

> Forgetfulness of self does not interfere with gratitude for His gifts. And for this reason: such forgetfulness does not lie in being unmindful of anything we possess, but rather in never confining ourselves to the contemplation of self, or dwelling upon our own good or evil in an exclusive or personal fashion. All such self-occupation severs us from pure and simple love, narrows the heart, and sets us further from true perfection by reason of seeking it in an excited, anxious, restless spirit, which comes of self-love.

> But though we may forget ourselves, that is to say, we may not be studying self-interest alone, we shall not fail often to see ourselves truly. We shall not contemplate self out of egotism, but as we contemplate God there will often be a sidelight, so to say, thrown upon ourselves; just as a man who stands looking at the reflection of another in a large mirror, while looking for that other man he beholds himself, without seeking to do so. And thus we often see ourselves clearly, in the pure light of God. The presence of God in purity and simplicity, sought after in very faithfulness, is like that large mirror, wherein we discern the tiniest spot that flecks our soul.

A peasant who has never passed beyond his own poor village only faintly realizes its poverty. But set him amid splendid palaces and courts, and he will perceive how squalid his own home is, how pathetic his rags, compared with such magnificence. Even so we realize our own loathsomeness and unworthiness when brought face to face with the beauty and greatness of God.

Talk as much as you will of the vanity and emptiness of the creature, the shortness and uncertainty of life, the inconstancy of fortune and friends, the delusions of grandeur, its inevitable and bitter disappointments, the failure of bright hopes, the vanity of all we attain, and the pain of the evils we endure. All these things, true and fair as they are, do not touch the heart; they do not reach far, or alter a man's life. He sighs over the bondage of vanity, yet does not seek to break his bonds.

But let one ray of heavenly light penetrate within, and forthwith beholding the depth of goodness, which is God, he likewise beholds the depth of evil, His fallen creature. Then he despises himself, hates, shuns, fears, renounces self; he throws himself upon God and is lost in Him. Thus it is that "one deep telleth another." Verily that man's loss is a blessed one, for he finds himself without seeking. He has no more selfish interest, but all turns to his profit, for everything turns to good to those who love God.[21]

This passage refers to a different kind of self-hate. It is actually a spiritual quality, but it relates to what we have been talking about. One often discovers in psychological studies that the very factors which lead to difficulties and disaster can be turned around to become the foundation and source of renewed health. If in the midst of our self-hate we face the fact that God loves us and if we don't back away from this mystery, we will receive a revelation of divine love which goes quite beyond anything we ever expected. A remarkable altruism will begin to emerge in the life of the person who has been delivered from self-hate. God's love will cascade down and heal him. God's love and concern will transform his rejected self.

The other meaning of "love of God" is our love for him. We come to realize that in the depths of our being there is an opening up to God, a love for him. Yet it is one of the basic teachings of the Church derived from Sacred Scripture that we cannot love God by our own strength. God must love himself within us. We have neither the ability, the capacity, the freedom nor the strength to reach out to the love of God. When we realize the burden of self-hate that we have been delivered from, we begin to love God in a new way. In Msgr. Ronald Knox's translation of the psalms we read, "I will love you, O Lord, and keep your name in honor, because of the greatness of the love that you have had for me in rescuing me from the depths of Hell."

Our love for God, a human love which has its origins in grace, begins with the deep personal realization that we were lost and that there was nothing lovable about us. Then we come to the stark and dreadful realization of our own self-hate. It is painful in proportion to the depth of our realization. Perhaps this is why the saints suffered so much. They had to come into contact first with their own weakness, then with their self-hate, and finally with their love of God.

Most people don't realize that St. Francis of Assisi, that beautiful and cheerful saint, struggled all his life with his own self-hate. He punished himself. He denied himself. He often thought he might be lost. He worried about his salvation for most of his life. That is why his heart was filled with gratitude.

St. Francis

The life of St. Francis was marked by a powerful conflict with his father. History has been hard on his father, making him a caricature of avarice and severity. The fact is that Francis would have bothered most fathers. His fun-loving personality had its melancholy side. Early on there were signs that he was trying to cope with self-hate. His need to identify with the outcast, the poor and the sick, despite his fastidiousness, is a sign of a person who knows self-hate. In all of this Francis heard the divine call addressed to him in the suffering of the Crucified. His secret is not that he received the call of God—we all do—but that he responded to it with all his heart, mind and soul.

We can estimate the depth of Francis' self-hate by several things: his constant disparaging references to himself, his utter lack of care about his appearance or health, his severe penances, and his fear of being lost. But nothing shows it better than his identification with lepers. He was most at home with them.[22]

It would be foolish indeed to measure the holiness of this man whose life has deeply moved millions of people for hundreds of years by his self-hate alone. But it is not at all inappropriate to look into his psychological makeup to find the sources of energy whereby he responded to the cross. His life powerfully demonstrates how the love of God can transform a weakness into a strength, a pathology into an opportunity for victory. Francis' part in his own sanctification was that he responded completely, lovingly to God. At the end of his days the miracle of the stigmata was completely in keeping with his personality and struggle with self-hate. Of all the signs of holiness that could have been given, this one emphasizes that hate can be transformed into love.

You and I should take refuge in God's love for us from the icy blast of self-hate. Repeatedly we must remind ourselves that God has first loved us. It is extremely important for our growth to be deeply aware that God loves us. We should also be messengers of God's love to those who hate themselves. There are many people around who are filled with self-hate because they are unaware of God's love.

If I tried to link the struggle for mental health with the struggle for holiness, I would say it is most clearly seen in the terrible battle against self-hate in the depths of the soul. Once the chain of self-hate is broken, the individual becomes free to love others, to be generous, to escape from his own darkness. This is part of the mystery of God's love. God has first loved us; let us begin now to love him.

The newly graduated young scientist whose letters I quoted earlier in this chapter, and who has now basically won the battle over self-hate, wrote these powerful words to me in the midst of his dark struggle: "The intensity of my self-hate, bitterness and confusion leaves me without a sense of my own control. The situation is not hopeless. We know too much about Christ, his mercy, his grace and his wisdom to cast aside all hope. Our one point of anchor is Christ. Even in my sorrow I still do not doubt this. We must learn to trust him. Trust."

Readers may wonder what happened to this distressed young person. We went through a long time of prayer and long-distance phone calls. Gradually through a combination of insight, acceptance, will power, and the action of divine grace, the force of self-hate was considerably diminished. It is my hope that in the course of time the pain he endured may be very productive in preparing him to help other people in their own difficult struggles. In fact he now has a very promising future in which "our sorrow may be turned into joy."

Chapter VII

Pride, Vanity and Love of God

Pride

Pride is the beginning of all sins and faults. According to the Book of Genesis it was a desire to be equal to God that led to the fall. And following hints in Scripture, the Fathers of the Church believed that the fall of the angels was caused by pride. They speculated that it was the pride of the angels which caused them to refuse to acknowledge the divinity of the second person of the Blessed Trinity when they foreknew that he was to become a creature of this earth. They simply could not endure that the Son of God would be a weak and limited human being. To borrow a phrase from St. Augustine, they could not bear to see omnipotence become tired, eternal beatitude weep, and life die. They could not abide the knowledge of the Incarnation, and, so it is said, they revolted. No one knows for sure, but it is an interesting speculation. Certainly the disciples of Satan in this world have been singularly characterized by pride. For examples we have only to look at the enemies of religion in the twentieth century. And it is obvious that when true religion goes off the track it is the result of pride.

There is something satanic about pride. It is the first fault, the first sin, the opening insult. But there is also something terribly ridiculous about pride. Pride is unquestionably the funniest sin. Have you ever seen the fellow as proud as a peacock walking around trying to get everyone else to acknowledge his importance? It is hard to keep a straight face. I am always waiting for the platform to collapse, or the fellow to fall over his own feet, or something else. It is such a ridiculous sin that even the angels must laugh at it sometimes.

Yet, though we laugh at the pride of others, we all have our own pride. How many times have we said to God: "What right have you to demand this of me? How can you ask this of me? Why did you allow this or that to happen to me? How could you do that? I am so good. I am one of the chosen, one of God's little boys and girls." Don't we all say these things? And that is pride. It is the pride of the scribes and Pharisees. And don't worry, we won't get into as much trouble as they did, as long as we are willing to accept the humiliations that God sends our way to cure our pride. They will be many. One of the special days of my life came when Cardinal Cooke asked me to be a liaison between the Missionaries of Charity of Calcutta and the archdiocese of New York. What an honor, I thought. The job proved to be one of my great failures in life. You try coordinating a flight of swans and a twenty-mule team and you will see what I mean. Mother Teresa once said to me, when I lost one of our charitable arguments over policy, "Well, how do you feel about the whole thing?" I replied, "As I usually feel—humiliated, but, unfortunately, not humbled." She answered, "Cheer up! Humiliation could be a road to humility." God kindly provides us with many of these little chances for improvement.

Pride sneaks down into the bottom of our soul. It makes us believe that we are something more than a creature. Pride makes us demand the things that are God's. It says, "I will not serve," or, "I will serve, but only under these circumstances," or, "I am willing to do everything you want, God, but could I make a suggestion? I'll carry the cross, but preferably something with wheels on one end, and a nice little shoulder pad." All these things are pride. While they may not be mortal sins of pride, they could grow into them.

If you have ever been a gardener in New York State, you know that no matter what you do, you will get poison ivy. You don't know where it comes from, but it is there. Life is a constant struggle against poison ivy and pride. Unfortunately, we can be seriously tempted by pride to the end of our lives. The old Irish proverb that the higher we climb, the higher the devil climbs, is true with regard to pride. Until the day we die it can trip us up. If we have a terminal illness, we can accept it as Cardinal Cooke did, calling it "a grace-filled moment," or we can rage against God. And that is pride. In the depth of our being the germ of pride will remain until we enter eternal life. And so, it is wise at least to be aware that there is a voice within us that says, "I will not serve."

At the end of the circus train of pride is a funny-looking caboose. It is painted somewhat like the fun-house at an amusement park. Of all forms of pride it is the least dangerous and most ridiculous. It is called vanity.

Vanity
Pride is a terrible sin, whereas vanity is the most venial of sins. It grows out of our childhood need to be recognized, to be someone. It is always hiding in the back of our minds like a little organ grinder's monkey showing off its new green hat, which it didn't make or earn. Vanity is the peacock showing off the feathers that it didn't create. I am writing this conference in New York City, the vanity capital of the world, where occasionally newspaper articles describe an event at which one of the designers shows off next year's fashions. "Is this going to be next year's style?" I gasp in

astonishment. "Dear Lord, will women look like that next year?" I ask myself. But they never do.

Early one evening, however, I saw a lady dressed in some of these clothes. Her husband looked like an undertaker, wearing a dark-blue suit, and appeared elegant but drab. But the lady looked as if she had butterfly wings on garments that scarcely shielded her from the spring breeze. These clothes may have cost several thousand dollars, but I wouldn't put them in the Thanksgiving collection, because they would be of no help to the needy. This poor lady looked very proud of her attire. Yet all I could think of was little birds that gather pieces of glass and other glittering objects, and take them back to decorate their nest.

But there is vanity on the poor people's scale as well. A girl once told me that she used to get out of the school bus in front of a neighbor's house because it looked so much nicer than her own. That is easily forgiven. Every once in a while someone will come up to me and say, "Oh, aren't you Fr. Benedict? I listen to your tapes." The reply in the depth of my being is, "I have nothing to do with those tapes at all. I have as little to do with them as the organ grinder's monkey has to do with the music the organ grinder makes." But the little bird of vanity comes by out of the circus train and I take a big deep breath and say, "Oh, somebody noticed." Feeling vanity over being noticed is not a mortal sin, but it is a venial sin. And if you don't consent to it, it is at least a temptation. In any case it is embarrassingly ridiculous.

There are even people who are vain about being totally miserable. Everything has gone wrong, so they make a career out of being the "sad sack" of their generation. They bear tragedy as someone else might wear a royal emblem or a purple heart

The danger of vanity is that it leads to greater temptations. These are the distractions of life, including self-importance, hypersensitivity, narcissism and the need for recognition. I don't mean distractions at prayer. I refer to unimportant things that we decide are terribly necessary for our ego to survive. We need this, that, or the other thing. So many times we work very hard only in order to receive a bit of recognition. When someone gives me recognition, I say, "I wish they didn't notice, because it makes me feel worse." Everyone of us, except the saints, goes through life with a little voice in our mind saying: "I need recognition. I need thanks. I need affirmation." Most of the time this is not even a sin, but it is the root of a sin. The sin is to lose peace of mind, and to forego any attempt at humility or generosity because others didn't notice. The sin is to lose track of the search for holiness.

If you no longer feel the need to be recognized, if you work very hard to get something done and it doesn't bother you that no one cares, you have made considerable spiritual progress. But if you are still struggling like most of us and a slight comes your way, take a deep breath, smile, and try to put up with it. This will prepare you to grow closer to the kingdom of God and not be distracted by vain things.

All around us things call out for recognition. All around us things say to us, "I am important for you. You must get me. Before you die you must have a taste of this or that, or when you die your life will be incomplete." It makes no difference how important the thing really is. In little country towns men fight as fiercely to become aldermen as those in other circumstances fight to become president of the United States. Trying to be chief usher in a small parish can be as spiritually dangerous for some people as trying to be emperor can be for others. Although we have the illusion that these things are important, they are not. They pass away.

There is an interesting historical parable about vanity. In Vienna the emperors of the Austro-Hungarian Empire are buried in a Capuchin friary. I suppose it was considered the humblest place to be buried. And when the funeral of the emperor took place the procession would go from St. Vitus Cathedral down to the Capuchins. The grand duke would ceremoniously knock on the locked doors of the friary. A little window would open and the superior would say, "Who is it?" The duke would answer something like this: "Franz Joseph, emperor of the Holy Roman Empire, king of Hungary, margrave of such and such." The superior would say, "We don't know him." So he'd knock again. "Who is there?" "Franz Joseph, his most Catholic imperial majesty, elector of the Pope, etc." The answer would come again, "We don't know him." The duke would knock a third time and the superior would say, "Who is there?" Then the grand duke would say, "Franz Joseph, a wretched sinner who seeks a place to lay his bones." Then the door would open. Only in death do some of us face the need to divest ourselves of the world's vanity. It would be wonderful if we could get over our sensitivities sooner.

A certain sensitivity is almost necessary for those who walk in the spiritual life. But we can be too sensitive, not only toward others, but even toward God. Our hearts become like little antique chapels in which we think that God must do something for us. When King Louis XIV lost some battle, he was heard to remark: "Does not God realize how much I have done for him?" Perhaps there is a touch of this vain sensitivity in all of us.

Make an inventory of your distractions. In one of his early books, Thomas Merton suggests that we start picking out of our hearts all the useless things that stand in the way.

Our Lord teaches us in parable after parable to be generous, give ourselves away, and carry the cross. He invites us to do this in the most direct way. His purpose is not only to encourage generosity, but also to help us get over our egotism and narcissism. Egotism and narcissism don't just distract us; as St. Paul warns, they lead us to envy, aggravation, arguments, backbiting and hatred.

Humility

What is the antidote to pride and vanity? Humility is the opposite, but it is an elusive virtue. You cannot seek it directly. You can decide to be generous. You can pray for hope and faith, which are gifts of God. You can struggle to be chaste, kind, understanding, and forgiving, but you really can't struggle to be humble. Once you think you are attaining it, you have lost it.

I used to get annoyed with people who talked about "learned Jesuits." For years I looked for a Jesuit who was not learned, and one day I met one. He was a lovely man: humble, simple—and dense. It was a real find. But just as people talk about learned Jesuits, they also unfortunately talk about humble Capuchins. I assure you, some of us Capuchins are not humble at all. Humiliated we may be, but humble? That's a different question. A famous Capuchin once advised us to be careful to protect the humility for which our Order was well known. That was the end of humility right there. It packed up and left. Although you can struggle to be a learned Jesuit, you really can't battle your way to be a humble Capuchin. Learning is an achievement of the intellect. Humility is a gift of grace. Consequently, there are probably more proud Capuchins than there are dense Jesuits.

What a wonderful thing it is to meet a humble Jesuit. And I have known many. As a boy I used to go to St. Ignatius Loyola Church where the Jesuit Fathers formerly lived in the most miserable circumstances. One of them was Teilhard de Chardin. He lived in this old rickety place and they had to move him out when they rebuilt it. So I have no intention of writing about humility. I would not want to be accused of hypocrisy.

The Love of God
The quality which helps us most to move toward humility and away from pride is the love of God. As we mentioned, the phrase "love of God" can mean two things. Here I refer to God's love which surrounds us. I am not convinced about our love for God. It doesn't impress me. Some people, especially the recently converted, are likely to be very impressed by the fact that they love religious things. They like to go to church and to pray. When they meditate, their heart may be curiously warmed. God seems very close to them. These things have happened to me and, regrettably, have co-existed very comfortably with my sins. The sins and prayers get all mixed together. No, our love of God is not very great.

The saints made little of their love for God. St. Simeon in one of his writings said. "I do not love God. I love myself. I do not worship God. I seek my own. I know nothing about the love of God." St. Francis was filled with fear of hell because he felt he did not love God enough. He cried, "Love is not loved." If you are preoccupied with analyzing your love for God but you haven't gone far on the spiritual journey, the Holy Spirit will let you know how little you love God. Does this sound terribly discouraging? Perhaps this painful awareness clears the way for something unspeakably important. Perhaps it lays the very foundation of the spiritual life, namely, the conscious, vibrant, powerful realization that God loves us. The First Epistle of

St. John stresses the great Christian teaching that God has first loved us. Not only in terms of time but even now, when we try to love him, his love for us comes first. Our love for him is merely a response.

There is a line in Sacred Scripture, "Deus ignis consumens." God is a consuming fire. We are consumed when we try to follow him. First our distractions are consumed. The thousands of distractions that plague us are swept away, and we come to care much less about recognition or self-fulfillment. We are drawn toward the powerful furnace of God's love. The fathers of Vatican Council II taught that the gifts of the Holy Spirit are given without regard to rank. Perhaps, if anything, rank and importance can be obstacles to the love of God. This is why you should pray for the clergy. We may have more obstacles to holiness than other people do. We could be foolish enough to take ourselves seriously and think we have a special place in God's sight. However, God loves everyone—Pope and pauper—equally.

Because God is infinite his love is like sunlight. It does not divide. You can not divide the sunlight itself. It is all the same. You can hide from it or stand in the shadows, but you do not affect the source of light itself. One could say that in a certain sense, God loved Judas Iscariot as much as he did the Blessed Virgin, because he loves us all infinitely. The difference is that the Blessed Virgin Mary opened her heart completely to God and Judas closed his heart. But did God cease to love him? The last time that Judas was with Christ, our Lord said to him, "Judas, are you betraying the Son of Man with a kiss?" The love of God is like an infinite river. Julian of Norwich says the love of God flows like a huge tranquil river. Like the Mississippi or the Hudson, it flows with an irresistible power, and its deep current is unhindered. You and I are in the river of

God's love. If we swim with the tide, we will float along
with that love. It will bring us to where we are supposed to
be. Then we will not be distracted, nor troubled by pride.
But as soon as we resist, even a little, our going gets rough
as though we are going against a river. First there are rip-
ples, then waves. Suddenly there are cataracts of white
water. We stand like rocks in the way of the great river.
While we don't stop the river of Divine Love, we create a
terrible turbulence all around us.

It is important to keep before your mind the river of
Divine Love. The human race built dams against this river,
but our Savior himself came and opened the floodgates. As
it flows to us in that great river, God's love is dyed with
blood, the precious blood shed by Christ. St. Paul says,
"Oh, the depth of the riches of the wisdom and knowledge
of God. How inscrutable are his judgments, how unsearch-
able his ways!" None of us can estimate how much God
loves another person, how much love he extends even to
his bitterest enemies.

We all become discouraged and tired at times. If you
try to carry the cross behind Christ, don't be surprised if
you fall. You won't fall three times; you'll fall three thousand times. Our journey to God is not like the Via Dolo-
rosa, our Lord's way to Calvary. Our journey lasts a lifetime. Over and over we fall, bruised and hurt. But we must
go on. St. Paul tells us that what urges us on is the love of
Christ.

I have chosen to end our meditation on stumbling
blocks and stepping stones with a startling picture of a
strange and unusual saint. On the surface this man had little pride or self-love. Closer inspection reveals that there
was great pride and, consequently, the possibility of great
humility. Our saint was mentally ill. Most mental illness
represents a regression to infancy. The most devastating

component of mental illness is the fear and anxiety that place mentally ill persons at the center of their world. Some of the mentally ill, especially those who are paranoid, go through the streets saying to themselves, "Look at these foolish people. They are all running around and don't recognize that I am the most important person in the world. I am Napoleon (or Julius Caesar)." This is the response to fear, and it is at the heart of severe mental illness.

An Unlikely Saint

Can such a person become a saint? This is not an irrelevant question, because at least one has been canonized. A driven, frightened, sick man, he recognized his own inner arrogance and self-importance, and desired above all things to lose himself in the quiet isolation of a Trappist monastery. He took a step against his own paranoid importance. As a young man he left his home in northern France, and made his way from one Trappist monastery to another. He entered eleven in all and was dismissed from each one. The monks recognized his piety, but they also recognized his craziness. Once in the middle of the night, as the monks slept in the dormitory, our friend came down the middle aisle bouncing a huge cross. The poor monks regularly got up at two o'clock in the morning, and were not pleased with his banging through the dormitory.

The Carthusians gave him a chance, but that failed too. He then set out for Italy to become a monk there, but he never succeeded. He spent his life going from shrine to shrine, struggling with his strange lonely vocation. Little is known of his interior life, but by the age of thirty-five he might be wrapped in prayer for eighteen hours a day. The custodian of the church in Rome where he prayed testified during the process of beatification that he used to wait until the afternoon to sweep the corner of the church, because our friend would be elevated above the ground as he prayed. Janitors in Rome are not impressed at all. I offered the liturgy in that church and the janitor must have been a descendant of that man. If you see someone nonchalantly smoking a cigarette at the last judgment, know that he is a janitor from a church in Rome.

Our poor little beggar impressed people. Here and there in southern France, people remembered him, although they usually did not know his name. One time he stayed in a farmer's barn. In the morning the farmer lined up his many children to have the man pray over them, because he could see how devout he was. As the beggar was leaving he touched the smallest boy on the head and said a special little prayer. That little boy was the grandfather of St. John Vianney.

The great musician, St. Lucia Philippini, had founded an order in Rome, and the sisters at the motherhouse used to give our wandering beggar his meals at the back door, where today there is a statue to him. Everyone in Rome knew about him. In one place in Italy there is a Creed written on the wall of a house, very much like the Apostles' Creed, but with such delicate little phrases as, "Christ was born of the Virgin Mary and walked among us in peace." Our beggar wrote that himself to teach the simple people. When a powerful earthquake devastated the area this house was not affected at all. The people claimed that the Creed prevented any damage to the house.

The Roman children used to torment the man. In his early days they would throw stones and make fun of him, even though he was generous to them. He would beg food in the street and give it to other beggars when he himself was fasting. Ironically, it was the mocking youngsters who ran through the streets shouting, "The saint is dead, the saint is dead" the day he died. Pilgrims may visit the house of the barber Zaccarelli at No. 2 on the Via dei Serpenti where the saint died. Papal soldiers had to be called to the Church of Santa Maria dei Monte to control the crowds at his funeral. An American in a long dark robe (then a sign of a Protestant clergyman) came into the crowded church. The minister, Rev. John Thayer, of an eminent family, stood in line to see what was going on. Because he looked so distinguished the soldiers made way and he was able to walk past the body. As he stood at the casket, the minister was converted to the Catholic faith. He was the first American Protestant clergyman to become a Catholic priest.

In the beautiful church of Santa Maria dei Monte, at a side altar, are his relics and a statue of him in his hobo's clothes and knapsack. This is the tomb of St. Benedict Joseph Labré. I was fortunate enough as a novice to be given the name Brother Benedict Joseph. Years ago writers explained the case of Benedict by saying that he had an unusual vocation. That was true, but they were afraid to say what was more important, namely, that Benedict Joseph Labré was mentally ill.

Can a mentally ill person be a saint? God who is no psychologist will do what he will. Who is to say that God will not allow the great river of Divine Love to run through the soul and tormented mind of a mentally ill person? You and I struggle with our hurt feelings and our sensitivities, but we never struggle with the delusions of grandeur and persecution that can haunt the mentally ill. We can organize our lives, but this man, like so many we see in the streets, had no place to live. The first time he was in a bed in fourteen years was the day on which he died in the barber's house, April 16, 1783.[23]

I went with a group of young pilgrims to the house on the Via dei Serpenti. There is a plaque on the outside wall: "Into this building on the 16th of April 1783 was carried the dying beggar Benedict Joseph." It carries the date of canonization: the feast of the Immaculate Conception in 1881. The room where Benedict Joseph died is now a beautiful little baroque chapel, complete with a white marble statue of the saint as he lay dying in the barber's bed. Large glass-fronted reliquaries contain his hobo's rags, the mattress on which he died, his old shoes, his knapsack, his letter-writing case where he kept the parchment on which he had written to his parents, as well as his Bible, prayer book and the wooden rosary he wore around his neck. It is very moving.

What is the secret of Benedict Labré? He is, in a unique way, the witness of God's love for us. This poor broken soul had managed to swim in the ocean of Divine Love. He had to give up what he thought was so important, that is, his desire to be a Trappist monk. Oddly enough he is the only canonized Trappist. And yet he died a hobo. There are in the Trappist Order many unrecognized saints, but he is the only one canonized.

I think it is essential that we recognize in our hearts that God will be God. He will be himself. It says in Sacred Scripture, "Let God be true." Of course God is true, but is our reflection of God, our image of God within us, true? God is everything and we shall be something only when we allow him to be our everything. Pride gets in the way— pious pride that says "How good I am." How many times did our Lord warn those who were self-righteous, who thought they were special? They fulfilled the law, avoided sin, and fasted, but our Lord warned them that publicans and harlots would enter the kingdom of heaven before them. If you fall into sin, if you struggle with weakness, if you deal with temptation, if you have to put up with your own hurt feelings patiently, you have seized the opportunity to embrace God's love. St. Paul, who struggled with his own pride and arrogance, asks us, "What shall separate us from the love of God, which is in Christ Jesus, our Lord?"

St. Benedict Joseph's secret is that in his confusion and illness he had somehow found God's love. Whatever there was in this poor broken soul he had surrendered to God as best he could. Benedict had found God especially in the cross.

God's love is shown to us in our Lord Jesus Christ on the cross. Look at the cross and you will see what happens to his love when it comes into the world. The bright clear waters of Divine Love are dyed dark red with blood. Love suffers; love is in pain; love is outraged; love is rejected. But love triumphs because nothing is more powerful than love. For love is stronger than death and its fire is brighter than the fire of hell, and its flame is the flame of the Being of God. In my own painful struggle against pride and vanity I can do nothing more than turn my eyes away from myself and focus on the love of God.

If we catch a glimpse of the immensity of that ocean, which is the purest reality, if we step out of the brief moment of our life and look into the eternity of endless days, if we turn away from the things of this world which we consider important and see that the streets are rivers of Divine Love and that the sky is illumined not by sun or moon but by the love of the Lamb of God, then we will find peace. If we think of that city where the trees bloom and bear fruit twelve times a year as it says in Sacred Scripture, if we long for that city where there is neither mourning nor weeping nor crying anymore for all such things have passed away, then our distractions diminish. Our humiliations will be joy to us because they separate us from things that are not important. If we can think of the heavenly Jerusalem at times when we are humiliated or cast down or betrayed or broken-hearted, we will rejoice because God has first loved us.

Chapter VIII

Sadness, Sorrow and Joy

Sadness

Sadness is, unfortunately, a universal experience. It is a feeling that arises from our own personal loss, deprivation or failure. Since sadness is not the same as sorrow, we ought to distinguish one from the other by defining sorrow as a sense of grief over the pain or stress of another. Often sorrow and sadness come together, as they do when a loved one dies. This distinction may seem arbitrary, but it will help to clarify our discussion. We will define sadness then as a response to our own loss, and sorrow as a response to the loss or grief of another.

Sadness comes to the good and the bad, to the worthy and the unworthy, to the simple and the sophisticated. It can even have a paralyzing effect in animals when they lose a newborn offspring or experience cruel treatment. Sadness is a response to the loss of what we need, or at least of what we expected to receive.

Religious people sometimes fall prey to the delusion that they will be able to avoid sadness by reason of their faith and trust in God. The advice of St. Teresa of Avila, "Let nothing disturb you," leads them to believe that they may arrive at a state of detachment in which they will never again experience the sadness that is the lot of most human beings. It seems to me that this expectation is unrealistic.

While great saints at the height of their development may have gone beyond the experience of personal loss, most other people on the way to holiness do indeed feel grief, remorse and a profound sense of loss from time to time. Read the lives of the saints and you will find situations of sadness in their lives. The Little Flowers of St. Francis describes an incident when the saint is sitting in a garden weeping by himself. He was consoled through a mystical experience in which he heard an angel play a stringed instrument in the distance.

Our Lord often advised the apostles not to let their hearts be troubled, but he himself was troubled in the Garden of Olives. While we can debate whether this experience was pure sorrow, as when he wept over Jerusalem, or whether it was sadness and sorrow together, we cannot escape the fact that he experienced these emotions on the very night before his crucifixion. My definition of sadness and my understanding of Christ's humanity permit me—in fact, almost require me—to believe that some of what he felt that night was sadness. His agony involved grief over what was about to happen to him, to his human life, and to his work of establishing the infant Church.

Unfortunately, those who seek an escape from the normal sadness of life through prayer and religious practice often use the defense mechanisms of denial and repression to create a false sense of tranquillity. This only stores away the tears and anger for another day. Constant denial of the realities of the human situation can lead eventually to a profound sadness and depression, which often require therapeutic intervention and medication.

Life usually presents grief in stages. In between are periods of joy and blessing. Any realistic approach to life advises taking the bad with the good, and reacting to each situation according to values, beliefs and strengths. We all know people who survive dreadful losses and go on to live another day. They cope not by denying their grief, but by accepting it and living through it with faith and hope that a better day will come.

Most of us don't have to worry about denying our feelings of sadness. Long ago we learned—perhaps too easily—to live with them. Your problem, like mine, may be not in denying sadness, but in feeding it, living into it with too much energy. Many religious people have depressive sides to their personalities; they sing the Holy Week hymns all year long. The temptation to sadness is all the more attractive because it seems to be a more sophisticated emotion than unalloyed happiness. Educated people often vie with one another in making dolorous evaluations of the passing scene and in dire predictions.

Illness, personal misunderstanding, failure to achieve life goals, and alienation from friends all contribute to an abiding sense of sadness. The prayerful person will soon find that this sadness seeks an expression in prayer. Such prayer may not be found in books, nor fit most people's definition of prayer.

The following prayer of a chronically ill person gives an insight into how bitter such prayer can be.

The Prayer of One Very Ill

Lord, the day is drawing to a close and, like all the other days, it leaves with me the impression of utter defeat. I have done nothing for You: neither have I said conscious prayers, nor performed works of charity, nor any work at all, work that is sacred for every Christian who understands its significance. I have not even been able to control that childish impatience and those foolish rancors that so often occupy the place that should be Yours in the "no-man's land" of my emotions. It is in vain that I promise You to do better. I shall be no different tomorrow, nor on the day that follows.

When I retrace the course of my life, I am overwhelmed by the same impression of inadequacy. I have sought You in prayer and in the service of my neighbor, for we cannot separate You from our brothers any more than we can separate our body from our spirit. But in seeking You, do I not find myself? Do I not wish to satisfy myself? Those works that I secretly termed good and saintly dissolve in the light of approaching eternity, and I dare no longer lean on these supports that have lost their stability.

Even actual sufferings bring me no joy, because I bear them so badly. Perhaps we are all like this: incapable of discerning anything but our own wretchedness and our own despairing cowardice before the light of the Beyond that waxes on our horizon.

But it may be, O Lord, that this impression of privation is part of a divine plan. It may be that, in Your eyes, self-complacency is the most obnoxious of all fripperies, and that we must come before You naked so that You, You alone, may clothe us.[24]

This prayer of Marguerite Teilhard de Chardin, president of the Catholic Union of the Sick, and sister of the well-known Jesuit writer, is not without hope, but it is a hope born of pain and suffering. The prayer reminds me that a believer who is not experiencing sadness at a particular time must appreciate the profound expressions of sadness of others who are enduring severe trials. There must be a special place in purgatory for people who tell the suffering, "Cheer up. It's not so bad." Worse still is the mindless cliché, "I understand," if you really don't. If you have been through a particular sadness which you can realistically and honestly share with someone else, you may break through to that person's experience.

But be careful. I have lost children whom I raised. I can explain and share that with a grieving parent. But I have never lost a spouse. I have never been arrested and disgraced. Although I can share in the sadness of someone who is going through these problems, I must not tell them that I understand their particular grief. I do not. It is far better to be silent or quietly consoling than to say "I understand," when I really don't.

Sadness has to be lived through. Sacred Scripture offers many prayers that can help in time of sadness. They teach us to overcome it. Although we will consider how to overcome sadness later, there is a prayer that I would like to present here as a confrontation of sadness. Sacred Scripture attributes this prayer to Jonah the prophet when he was in the belly of the whale. Most of us have had a symbolic experience of being in the belly of the whale, that is, in a frightening situation that unexpectedly saves us from certain destruction. Being swallowed by the whale was Jonah's terror; it was also his deliverance.

Yahweh had arranged that a great fish should be there to swallow Jonah, and Jonah remained in the belly of the fish for three days and three nights. From the belly of the fish he prayed to Yahweh, his God. He said:

> I called to the Lord, out of my distress,
> and he answered me;
> out of the belly of Sheol I cried,
> and thou didst hear my voice.
> For thou didst cast me into the deep,
> into the heart of the seas,
> and the flood was round about me;
> all thy waves and thy billows
> passed over me.
> Then I said,
> "I am cast out from thy presence;
> how shall I again look upon thy holy temple?"
> The waters closed in over me,
> the deep was round about me;

weeds were wrapped about my head
at the roots of the mountains.
I went down to the land
whose bars closed upon me for ever;
yet thou didst bring up my life from the Pit,
O Lord, my God.
When my soul fainted within me,
I remembered the Lord;
and my prayer came to thee,
into thy holy temple.
Those who pay regard to vain idols
forsake their true loyalty.
But I with the voice of thanksgiving
will sacrifice to thee;
what I have vowed I will pay,
Deliverance belongs to the Lord (Jon 2:2–9).

Often we can pray only for the grace to survive. Expressions of fear and sadness, especially those addressed to God in prayer or shared with others, are usually helpful. Even bitter expressions may contain a desperate trust in God. Prayers or expressions of sadness "let off steam." They are a control valve for powerful emotions, and they win the grace of God.

Although sadness should not be overindulged, it must nevertheless be expressed. A sad person needs to find ways and means to express this emotion, not only in prayer but also in art, music, and such actions as mourning for someone who has died. To just get trapped in an expression of sadness is to feed and overindulge it.

When I was an altar boy, it was often my responsibility to accompany a priest to the cemetery. An old prayer which was recited at the grave often returns to me in times of sadness. "Let them languish not in fruitless and unavailing grief nor in sorrow as they who have no hope, but through their tears look meekly up to Thee, the God of all consolation."

To live through sadness is honest; to live on sadness is destructive. At times it is necessary to give oneself a good jolt and move on. This is where the poor people have an advantage. I have often participated in the funeral of a poor black or Hispanic person in the inner city. Sadness, sorrow and bitterness find their full expression at such a funeral. But eventually the need to survive demands that grief be left behind. The struggle to live goes on. The most unfortunate people are those who have the resources to indulge sadness for weeks, months, or years. In such cases concern for someone else who needs help may cause the sufferer to put his sadness aside.

I once knew a man who had lived through the most dreadful of horrors, the Holocaust. He survived the death camps of the Nazis only to live through an insurmountable sadness that lasted for years and went far beyond the sorrow he felt over the destruction of his family. He used his grief and sadness well to remind others that the horror could happen again if we did not accept responsibility for our collective guilt. But he himself lived on sadness. Then one day he had to give up some of his grief because God had given him a little daughter. Children cannot grow on a diet of pure sadness. They have to laugh, and so he changed for his child. He moved on. It was the other half of the beatitude, "How blessed are they who mourn, for they shall be comforted."

Sorrow

One of the noblest human emotions is sorrow, or grief, over the experience of another. Every compassionate figure in human history, every great saint, is known to have shared in the sufferings of others. Every truly human person is familiar with sorrow. Every thoughtful Christian must at times meditate on Christ as the Man of Sorrow, as one who is familiar with grief. The prophecies concerning Christ were filled with a tragic note and were fulfilled in the life of Jesus of Nazareth to an extent far beyond what could have been expected. A Christ without sorrow is a mockery—a false god at best. While there are religious figures, particularly in the Orient, who are presented as having arrived at a stage beyond sorrow, such a claim has never been made by Christians of their Founder. How could such a claim be made of one whose dying words include, "My God, my God, why have you forsaken me?"

Unfortunately, contemporary Christianity has tended to deny the reality of the cross by covering it with gold and jewels, or by hiding it where it can scarcely be found. Such denial is noticeable in many modern churches—perhaps as a symptom of the subconscious dread of nuclear war which causes people to deny the sorrowful element in life and in the Gospels. One is reminded of the czar who forbade Tchaikovsky to end his ballets on a tragic note, because his imperial patron had to live with such calamities and sorrows in everyday life.

Sorrow is inescapable. We all long for things that we cannot have in this life, especially for a love that cannot be lost. If we happen to go through times when we experience little personal grief and sorrow, there is the universal suffering around us. We are bound by our humanity and our faith to be part of that sorrow, to recognize that the mourner's bell rings for us. It ill becomes a Christian to act like those tourists who go to exotic lands but stay hermetically sealed in luxury hotels, so that they don't have to see and smell the poor who swarm around their beautiful paradise. Often what is quaint or rustic to the tourist represents severe need and the fruits of injustice done to the local inhabitants. The Christian must react in some compassionate way to the needs and sufferings of others and cannot afford to wall himself off emotionally.

Often the poor children who look with hungry eyes at the pleasure domes of the tourist trade are made even more unfortunate by the very trade the tourists bring. And when the poor rebel and follow leaders of vengeance and wrath, the tourists are surprised. They fail to comprehend that they themselves were part of the oppression they piously condemn. They failed to share in sorrow and hence they did not respond to it.

Sorrow is not only the great leveler of the rich and poor, but it is also the way one can understand and participate in the suffering of others, so that eventually there may be some change for the better. Eugene Debs, the nineteenth century socialist leader, summed this up very well in his final courtroom statement before he was unjustly condemned: "So long as any man is unjustly deprived of his legitimate wages, I am that man. So long as any man is unjustly imprisoned, I am that man." While we may not accept Debs' solution to the problem, we have to accept his sentiments, especially if we accept the Gospel.

Personal suffering and sorrow are the very things that can make intellectual convictions about justice and mercy take on a human dimension. Such writers as Dostoevski, Tolstoy, Dickens and Hemingway used not only their talents but also their personal sufferings to make society aware of human need and injustice. They appeal to the sorrow and compassion of their readers in order to build a bridge between the poor and those who are fortunate enough to have the leisure to read books.

There is a strange and often misunderstood problem here for organized religion and especially for the Church. Much of the world's sorrow comes from sin and misbehavior. The devout person who tries to lead an orderly life and fulfill his or her responsibilities is likely to experience less sorrow than the disorganized, irresponsible person. Religious practice and morality remove a person from a sizable portion of the world's sorrow. "Happy are they who walk according to the law of the Lord," and unhappy are they who do not. Unfortunately, this can lead the devout to be less sorrowful and, consequently, less compassionate than the poor sinners of the world. A number of Jesus' parables warn about this tendency. The saints, combatting their own possible complacency, purposely avoided the comfort of their virtuous lives by sharing in the misery begotten of sin. In any society the difference between the pious and the saintly is often the degree of compassion and acceptance of another's pain through sorrow that has strangely linked the saintly and the sinful.

We should not only cope with our own sorrows and learn from them, but we should also share in other people's sorrow and suffering, even if they have brought them on themselves.

The devout are often unprepared to understand the bitterness and helplessness of other people. The devout are seldom beaten, betrayed, sold into slavery, raped, or made the sport of others' vices. When these things do happen to the devout, there is usually outrage, a cry for justice, and sometimes social change. But the poor or the dependent often suffer in silence with no hope of justice. I have often been struck by the mute helplessness of unwanted girls who are given over to prostitution by a parent who neither wanted nor loved them. Most people think these girls have "gotten off the track." The fact is that they never had a track to be on in the first place. Their children are often as unwanted as they were. They are children of suffering and pain. The only link between these girls and me is an abiding sense of sorrow. I cannot really empathize with their view of life, since their experience is entirely different from my own. Sorrow alone is the bridge. I ask never to be delivered from that sense of sorrow. I ask only to let it consistently move me to do something else, something more, to relieve the sorrows of those I meet on my way through life.

Sorrow comes eventually into every life, and those who are familiar with it often discover that it can be a blessing. The sorrowful have a better chance of making progress and overcoming apparently insurmountable obstacles than those who experience relatively little pain and suffering. Sorrow is a stern teacher who can instruct us in maturity, patient endurance, and hope. Sorrow itself gives no hope, but it recruits hope, to borrow a phrase of Kierkegaard's who knew much about it. "Sorrow makes us reach out in hope if we have anything to hope for at all."

This is why sorrow has played so great a role in the pursuit of holiness for Christ's followers. Christianity has taught that suffering is a bitter waste unless it is joined with sorrow, that is, with suffering for others and with hope. Hope is an act of faith, made solely with the assistance of grace, which causes us to believe that God will give us and those who are dear to us the means of salvation. Hope and sorrow go together. Sorrow grieves for the sufferings of others in this world, and hope makes this grieving endurable. Consequently those who have hope must expect to endure more sorrow than others do, because they can go on, whereas others are simply numbed or destroyed by pain. Christian suffering is a unique combination of sorrow and hope. Its origins are the same as those of any other human suffering. It is akin to the suffering of any believer who hopes in God, but Christian suffering has a special component. It is linked with the mystery of Christ, the Man of Sorrow.

In the personal notes of Cardinal Cooke, the late arch-bishop of New York, I found the following lines on suffering:

> Suffering teaches us three things. It teaches us not to cling to this life but to keep our eyes on eternity. A person who has suffered will not fear death.
>
> Suffering teaches us to be compassionate to others who suffer.
>
> And, finally, suffering teaches us to unite all of our own pains to the suffering of Christ, our Lord, who suffered for us.

The suffering that seems to lack any purpose is the most destructive suffering. When transformed into sorrow through compassion for another and suffused with hope, suffering can give rise to great joy. There are innumerable misfortunes in life arising from accidents, the malice of others, and natural disasters. From automobile fatalities to birth defects, from the killing of the innocent to epidemics, human life is vulnerable to all sorts of things that cause suffering. Sorrow and hope, compassion, and a belief that God will bring good out of evil as he did in the life, death, and resurrection of Christ are the keys to a joy that the world cannot give.

Joy

Just as there are all kinds of suffering, so are there all kinds of joy. Joy finds an echo in the animal kingdom when we see puppies frolic or kittens purr. Human joy comes from the fulfillment of needs and desires for security and pleasure, or from the end of pain. Sadly, there are evil joys which, as Scripture says, cause men to rejoice at iniquity. This joy is usually described as adding a particularly wicked aspect to evil deeds, as if the natural goodness of joy should never have been corrupted by rejoicing at evil. The worst pictures in the Dachau concentration camp museum show soldiers laughing at the torments of their victims.

Apart from the joy of evil, which is a curse, there is a whole gamut of passing or ephemeral joys, some of which are good, like the joy of celebrating with friends. Some passing joys may be indifferent, like the joy of seeing your team win a game, and some may be sinful, like the joy of a thief. In the Gospel, our Lord warns us not to cling to passing joys. The parables of the rich farmer and of the rich man and Lazarus are among several warnings Jesus gives to his followers not to cling to earthly joys. We can and should experience joy at good things, and even consecrate indifferent good fortune with joyful thanksgiving to God. But such joys must always be kept in perspective.

The greatest joys are the things of the spirit and those that pertain to the desire for fulfillment that cannot fail. Everyone knows that true joy cannot tarnish or be taken away. Those who do not believe in the everlasting deny that such joy is actually possible. Thus they are ultimately pessimistic because they believe they can never find the joy that they seek the most.

For those blessed with some awareness of the work of the Spirit, great joy is possible. The angels said to the shepherds, "Behold I bring you tidings of great joy. A Savior is born for you." This great joy is surpassed finally by the joy of the apostles and disciples when they realized that the crucified Master had indeed returned from the dead. These are examples of spiritual joy which the world cannot give.

Unfortunately most of us—even most devout Christians—are not attentive to this great joy. We go perfunctorily about our duties, we live in close proximity to things that gave the saints the greatest joy, i.e., the Eucharistic Presence, the word of God, the knowledge of salvation, the joy of serving Christ in the poor, and we go among these things with little joy. I have been to religious gatherings that could easily have served as an advertisement for the League of the Militant Goddess. I've heard the Holy Spirit invoked at proceedings that he could have had nothing to do with, because joy is a sign of his presence.

Why is this? The question is not why Christ's followers suffer. They should. The question is why they have so little joy. Not only can joy co-exist with sorrow and suffering, it should make them endurable and holy. Who has not witnessed the rare joy and peace of a believer who faces a terminal illness with faith and hope? This joy, which is a gift of the Holy Spirit, is founded on the hope of eternal life. It can have an amazing effect on the healthy who have ears to hear and eyes to see.

Perhaps most unusual is the radiant joy of the martyrs. The accounts of martyrdom abound with stories of their joy at joining this most powerful witnessing to a faith in life after death, a salvation promised by God. Certainly there are many martyrs whose causes we do not agree with and whose death may seem to be little more than fanaticism for an empty or erroneous cause. And yet there is a psychological fact that cannot be avoided. The believer who is willing to give up his or her life for a cause will experience serenity and a mysterious joy at the moment of death. The origins of this joy certainly are their belief that they have traded what is passing for what is eternal. They have given up temporary joys for the hope and expectation of eternal joys. Our Lord himself speaks of this joy on more than one occasion. Perhaps the most powerful teaching he gives on this subject is to be found in John 16:20–22.

Most of us will never face martyrdom. We will, however, face the terrible sorrow that comes from the loss of someone we love. We will encounter sadness when our lives and potentials are diminished by sickness or premature death. Recent studies in developmental psychology indicate that even very successful people in later middle age are apt to experience a sense of failure. And what about the sorrow that comes from some irreversible calamity—an accident or severe illness that leaves someone dear to us physically or psychologically incapacitated?

We have all experienced some instant when our future suddenly takes a different turn. And then out of the darkness we are "surprised by joy," in C. S. Lewis' marvelous expression; "suddenly, unexpectedly God is there." He offers a way. Perhaps at first we are so angry and bitter that we don't want to see the way out or take it. Many in fact do this and never again find joy in their lives.

We hesitate. We refuse to be deceived again by the promise of happiness and peace. But something beyond us drives us on. We find in the darkness itself an answer to sorrow, a way out of tragedy. It is not a magical answer, but rather a way to make the darkness part of the answer that we must carve out of life with God's help.

The words of Psalm 139 have a new meaning:

Even the darkness is not dark to thee.
The night is bright as day.

The mystery of Christ is revealed in ways that are practical for our needs and sufferings. The mystery of Christ brought salvation and eternal hope out of the greatest tragedy and sinful injustice ever perpetrated by the fallen children of Adam. His final prayer, "Father, forgive them, for they know not what they do," brings hope not only to the worst sinners but also to the most devout Christians who realize with fear and trembling that along the way they may often have passed Christ, hidden in the disguise of the outcast.

The mystery of Christ has many aspects. None of them is more important than this: out of sin, suffering and pain, God's love, revealed in Christ Jesus our Lord, has brought hope and eternal life. This realization can bring the highest and most invincible joy to those who accept it. It is a joy that the world cannot take away. It is a joy that goes beyond even the joy of the martyrs.

The suffering and sorrow of the martyrs seems remote from our everyday lives. Even in suffering and sorrow our lives seem unimportant and can appear to have no meaning. But to God no suffering or sorrow is unimportant if it can be transformed by love. This love, shown to God or to those dear to us in him, has a transforming power. Through the gifts of the Holy Spirit love can bring joy into sadness and sorrow—and can eventually transform them into eternal joy.

The following true story movingly illustrates how grace can lead to victory over death. The sorrow of this girl and her family was very real. Her ultimate joy is what we must all hope for in our sorrow. This account is provided by Sister Lois Darold, principal of St. John's Villa Academy on Staten Island.

The Story of Felicia

Felicia Mangione was born with a hole in her heart. She lived under medical supervision during her first six years, after which the hole closed and she enjoyed a year of good health. During the summer between her second and third grades she was hit by a car. Her skull was fractured and she was in a coma for almost three weeks. The doctors could give no assurance of her recovery.

When Felicia came out of the coma, she assured her parents that she was all right. She spoke of having talked to Jesus. He told her that in this world there were too many people who were "takers," as far as God was concerned. He was asking her to be a "giver." For the next year she was in and out of hospitals for corrective surgery and eventually a plate was placed in her head. During this period she accepted uncomplainingly all that had to be done.

For the next five years Felicia developed as a "normal" young girl. She loved a challenge, never using her past illness as a crutch. Among her favorite pastimes were bicycle riding, horseback riding, and skating. She was active and involved, and served as a junior assistant to a local Brownie troop. In September 1984 Felicia entered St. John's Villa Academy on Staten Island, New York, as a freshman. Almost immediately she found her niche among the cheerleaders. Dedicated and enthusiastic, she was present at all practice sessions and made the time pass quickly with her gentle sense of humor. She worked hard at her studies, worried about exams, and shared hopes and dreams with her friends. Friends have described her as a quiet girl who made people laugh when things grew tedious. Her parents and neighbors remember her at this period as conscientious, sensitive to others, independent, fun-filled, and somewhat detached from material possessions.

In July 1985 the first symptoms of a new illness began to appear: tiredness and black-and-blue marks; finally one day Felicia lost consciousness. Her trip to the emergency room one July night and a subsequent visit to her doctor led to the diagnosis of aplastic leukemia.

Felicia and her parents now began the numerous trips to Manhattan hospitals, hoping that a variety of treatments would put the disease into remission. In September she was admitted to NYU Medical Center and placed in protective isolation. During this time she began to wrestle with God. Without turning away from him, she nevertheless experienced anger, confusion, and anxiety about the future and especially about missing school. She received cards, bouquets of flowers and balloons, teddy bears, and phone calls to say that she was not alone. There was an outpouring of prayers and words of encouragement.

In October the doctors recommended her transfer to the National Institute of Health Hospital in Bethesda, Maryland, in the hope that an experimental treatment might prove successful. Felicia's mother, Marie, went with her; she stayed in the hospital room and entered into her daughter's "journey" in a special way. During October and November Felicia underwent a series of treatments and constant transfusions. Her doctors, nurses, and hospital staff came to know her as the gentle girl with the soft smile who never complained. Whatever they had to do she accepted; at times she apologized if she moved during a procedure.

Members of the chaplain's office as well as a personal priest friend of the family began to visit Felicia regularly. They talked, prayed, and shared the Eucharist with her. During this period she seemed to be coming to terms with something within her spirit. Her mother would pray with and for her, but she said Felicia never offered to share her troubles and her mother did not press the issue. There were many offers to bring Felicia to the chapel, but she declined to go, although she never resented her mother or other family members going. At some point, Alice, the Protestant hospital chaplain, passed along to Felicia a little book of thoughts, prayers and reflections edited by a Franciscan priest. Felicia opened it to the poem "The Weaving." Her mother recalls Felicia's deep impression with the poem, which she read often. She confided in her mother, saying "Mom, God has finally spoken to me." When she could no longer read for herself, Felicia would ask her mother to read the poem to her. It began to give her a sense of peace and consolation. This poem, written by an unknown author, is the key to understanding the great spiritual step this girl took as her physical life ebbed. It is the step of absolute trust.

THE WEAVING

My life is but a weaving
Between my God and me;
I may not choose the colors,
He knows what they should be;
For He can view the pattern
Upon the upper side,
While I can see it only
On this, the under side.

Sometimes He weaveth sorrow,
Which seemeth strange to me;
But I will trust His judgment,
And work on faithfully;
'Tis He who fills the shuttle,
He knows just what is best;
So I shall weave in earnest
And leave with Him the rest.

At last, when life is ended,
With Him I shall abide,
Then I may view the pattern
Upon the upper side;

Then I shall know the reason
Why pain with joy entwined,
Was woven in the fabric
Of life that God designed.

On December 8, one of the sisters of St. John the Baptist (the congregation which runs the high school) was professing her perpetual vows. Sister Ann Francis knew about Felicia and had been praying for her. She was asked to pray for Felicia in a special way on her profession day and promised to do so. Marie was informed of the upcoming event and said she had been praying especially to the Blessed Mother. I recall now that Sister Ann Francis asked me to remember this girl and her family at the Mass I celebrated on the feast of the Immaculate Conception. Little did I expect to preach about this girl someday.

On Friday, December 6, a priest friend came to pray with Felicia and bring her Communion. Afterward, she dropped into a sleep and seemed to have a terrible nightmare. During Friday and Saturday, whenever Felicia slept she seemed to be engaged in a strong struggle within her spirit. On the morning of Sunday, December 8, she awoke and appeared to have found a peace that even her illness could not disturb. From then on she began to ask to visit the chapel and surprised everyone by the amount of time she spent there in quiet prayer. On more than one occasion when someone tried to bring her back to her room, she asked for more time, stating, "I haven't finished talking to him yet." Or simply, "I'm not ready, I'm still praying." During the time in chapel, she seemed oblivious to her pain.

Around this time Felicia was quite taken with concern for another young girl suffering from the same illness. She prayed for her often. When her mother questioned why Felicia never prayed for herself, for healing, she replied: "I can't. God wants me to be a giver." During December, Felicia's strength began to fail. The hopes of remission were fading as treatments became more frequent. Those who attended her during her last weeks attest to her unfailing courage, her gentle faith, and her quiet trust in God. She was a source of faith and strength to those who came into contact with her. As her body grew weaker, her spirit seemed to grow stronger. And always she expressed a concern for those around her, especially her parents and brother.

On the morning of December 31, Felicia refused to take any medication, simply saying, "No more now." Having celebrated Christmas with her family, she now began to lose more of her physical capabilities, including partial vision and the energy to speak much. Her immediate family was with her on this last day of the year and witnessed her failing condition. Later, they shared with one another the fact that at different times that day they had gone to chapel and asked God to release her from her suffering. Felicia died at 9:30 P.M.

Sister Lois' account of Felicia's life and death demonstrates how an ordinary person can deeply influence the lives of others. Felicia's early death brought the most profound sorrow to her parents, family and friends. Her mother has explained: "She was not only my daughter, she was my friend." But Felicia's death was also a profound message for many in her circle of friends and acquaintances, and for those who read this book. It proclaimed an unshakable faith and hope in this life, and, beyond it, in a life with God.

A young life taken away is cause for deep sorrow. A death overcome by everlasting life is filled with a joy that this world cannot give. Such a joy is never easily won. In

Felicia's life it was won by pain, struggle, prayer and generosity. Through her efforts she came to an honest acceptance of her impending death. She looked with new eyes at the "weaving" of her life, knowing that God alone sees the other side. This won for Felicia the opportunity to be an encouragement to other people in their sorrow. Little did John and Marie Mangione realize the depth of meaning that the name of their little girl would have. Felicia means joy. In their case, it meant sadness and sorrow mingled with joy as they followed their little girl in the wheelchair into the chapel where Christ awaited her with a joy that no one can take away. Someday their joy will also be complete.

> So you have sorrow now,
> but I will see you again
> and your hearts will rejoice,
> and no one will take your joy from you (Jn 16:22).

Epilogue

Pain Is Not Unhappiness

In recent years it has been popular and at times helpful for writers to offer solutions to spiritual difficulties drawn from psychology and clinical techniques. It must be obvious to the reader that in this series of meditations I have endeavored to do the opposite. In exploring apparent psychological problems, I have tried to draw answers from the teachings of faith and Christian tradition—especially the Gospel. My purpose has been not to imply that the first process—namely, seeking psychological solutions—was erroneous. Rather my intent has been to examine the impact of Christian revelation and personal faith on the conflicts and difficulties of life.

In following this course I must acknowledge my debt to Professor Viktor Frankl who pointed the way in his work *Man's Search for Meaning*. However, Dr. Frankl did not endeavor to use solutions drawn from the Gospel or Christian revelation, because he was—and assures me he still is—Jewish in his belief. For answers to life Frankl drew very effectively from his own experience of God during the Holocaust. I have drawn mostly from the experience of others and sometimes from my own. I have obviously based this book on the Christian message contained in the Gospel. The religious experience of one who believes in a personal God—the God of Abraham and of St. Paul—is one that unites human needs and divine gifts in a dynamic relationship, one that constantly grows and changes, one that can seem harmonious or conflicted, peaceful or dark. All our potentials and negative possibilities, our human capabilities and limitations come into play in a manner that resembles Jacob's wrestling with the angel. From such experiences we emerge changed and often wounded. If our personal experience is an authentic one in which there is more truth than illusion, the change will always be in the direction of growth and maturation, of coming to full stature in Christ.

We are incapable of achieving our desired destiny by ourselves because of the innate limitations of human nature, because of the wounds that derive from the mysterious reality of original sin, and because our hearts are restless to possess the transcendent God.

The revelation of Christ and our adoption by God that was won by his blood are essential if we are to achieve our eternal goal. Our peace in this world requires that we actually, even forcefully, live our lives in the light of that revelation.

Spiritual maturity for the Christian requires a constant energetic struggle to overcome moral faults and to behave according to the teachings of the Gospel and the Christian tradition. It demands an intellectual struggle to come to an ever-new knowledge of the mystery of Christ in our own lives and in our relationship with others, including strangers and enemies who represent Christ to us. Finally, our spiritual journey must be marked by trust and hope that God providentially gives us the things necessary for salvation. This knowledge will sustain us in the mishaps of life, in the circumstances of the physical world and in the operation of natural forces.

As the Christian world vision is achieved by mind and heart, by intelligence and will constantly assisted by grace, the meaning of life as a journey toward the Father's house begins to grow clear. Pain, suffering, illness, rejection, failure and death fall into a new perspective. Life begins to be seen as a difficult journey through a vale of tears.

Admittedly, the need for a sense of humor, the need to laugh, is accentuated by this knowledge, because the tears would be overwhelming if it were not for life's absurdities and jokes. Those who know how to endure pain will know how to laugh in spite of it all.

Once in my life, early in the 1970's, having inadvertently bought the superficial humanism of the moment, I gave up (I am ashamed to admit) the recitation of the Salve Regina (the "Hail, Holy Queen"). The reference to life as a valley of tears and as an exile seemed not to be in keeping with the spirit of those palmy days. Then one evening I suddenly faced the most shattering experience of my life. A troubled youngster with whom I had worked for ten years slipped into insanity and took his own life. I stood in the dark city street in front of our boys' home and there echoed in my soul the old prayer, "Mourning and weeping in this valley of tears, and after this, our exile, show unto us the Blessed Fruit of thy womb, Jesus." On that dark night the mystery of Christ was revealed to me as never before.

Afterward I did some research on this remarkable prayer and discovered that it had been written almost a thousand years ago by a man who was born so deformed that he could never stand. The author, Blessed Herman, lived forty painful years in the German Benedictine monastery of Reichenau. He was a genius who wrote a number of scientific studies, even though his speech was so impaired that he was difficult to understand. Herman eventually went blind and turned his talent to writing hymns and poems. The Salve Regina, which ends this book, is his masterpiece and has been recited billions of times since his death, bringing hope and joy to those who prayed it in dark times.

A few years ago I met a remarkable young man, Dr. William Barton Hurlbut, who is a physician, poet, and composer and is also an admirer of Blessed Herman. He shared with me his own story of a stumbling block that became a stepping stone. He also shared his beautiful lyric poem, which is really a hymn in honor of Blessed Herman. I can think of no better way to end this book than to let Dr. Hurlbut, an expert on medical ethics, tell his own story and sing his hymn.[25]

I Knew Our Lives Would Never Be the Same

During my years as a medical student, I studied under world-renowned scientists. My biochemistry teacher, Paul Berg, won the Nobel Prize for his work in recombinant DNA, and others were conducting equally dramatic research in embryology and brain chemistry. I could see that a revolution in our understanding of biology was beginning and that it offered great hope for curing disease, but it also had disturbing implications.

In my senior year I helped set up Stanford's first course in medical ethics and I accepted a post-doctoral fellowship to study theology and medical-moral problems.

One week after I graduated from medical school, my wife had our first child. The labor was long and there were problems in delivery. The obstetrician decided to do an emergency Caesarean section. By the time we got to the operating room, there was no fetal heartbeat. We scrubbed our hands for the required seven minutes to avoid infection, knowing that every second meant more damage to the baby. When the little girl was finally born, she was limp and pale. I think I heard the resident physician say, "She's dead," but they tried to resuscitate her. After almost ten minutes, they managed to get her heart beating and then rushed her to the infant intensive-care unit. She had gone without oxygen for an incredibly long time.

I remember driving home from the hospital in the early dawn with tears streaming down my face. All I could do was call out to God. Because of the lack of oxygen, our baby had severe seizures and cerebral palsy. She might never walk, talk, or even sit up.

I knew our lives would never be the same, and there were moments when I wondered whether it might have been better if the child had died. But above all my wife and I hoped for life. We prayed for God's healing but especially for the grace to love unconditionally the child he had given us. We knew that she was God's invitation to us to grow in love, to become more like Christ.

And then a wonderful transformation took place in our hearts. I had always had a certain dread and fear of having a handicapped child. Now I realized that such a burden could also be rich in joy. It had brought us into the very heart of life.

I remembered St. Francis: one day he met a leper and gave him a coin; then, in spite of his enormous dread of leprosy, he embraced the man, desiring to love him just as Christ loves each of us. He later said that from that moment on, all his dread became the source of great sweetness. He had overcome his deepest fear. Now the sick and the poor, the unlovely and unloved, were his brothers and sisters. Regardless of their circumstances, he treated all people with courtesy, as beloved of God.

That radiant love was the most beautiful gift of all. How I hoped that my little injured child would receive such respect and courtesy as she went through life.

By the grace of God she has been greatly healed. By all medical standards it has been an extraordinary healing. The seizures stopped, the spasticity steadily declined, and we were able to take off her leg braces. Now she is a happy,

active child going to a normal school. She has some difficulties, but her handicap is relatively mild.

But as with all Christ's healing miracles, there was
more than physical healing. Our daughter's healing was like
a window that permitted us to view the beauty and mystery
of God and his plan for salvation. I would never have
hoped for such an experience, and yet it has been one of the
deepest, most transforming blessings of my life.

I am so grateful to be a Christian and united in faith
with those who, throughout history, have stood up for the
weak and abandoned—like the early Christians who res-
cued the unwanted infants from the garbage heaps of
Rome.

I think we are at a crucial point in history. Advancing
biotechnology will allow us to manipulate the basic fabric
of human life. We will be tempted to use our knowledge as
an extension of our vanity and pursuit of pleasure. There
will be pressures to intervene in genetics and embryological
development to produce desired physical and mental char-
acteristics. And I fear that the view of the body as a com-
plex machine, which is so helpful to scientific investigation,
is leading to an incomplete, perverse vision of human life.

I remember an incident one day when my daughter
was first starting to talk. She had fallen down and came in
to tell us she had hurt herself, but she said, "Mommy, my
self hurts." That little *self* in there, that mystery of flesh and
spirit present from conception! That sacred image of God!

What great good lies ahead if we can use our medical
knowledge with tenderness and mercy—with a tenderness
that sees the wonder and sanctity of life, and a mercy that
recognizes in suffering an opportunity to grow richer in
love.

HERMAN THE CRIPPLE

by William Barton Hurlbut, M.D.

I am least among the low,
I am weak and I am slow;
I can neither walk nor stand,
Nor hold a spoon in my own hand.

Like a body bound in chain,
I am on a rack of pain;
But He is God who made me so,
that His mercy I should know.

Brothers, do not weep for me!
Christ, the Lord, has set me free.
All my sorrows He will bless;
Pain is not unhappiness.

From my window I look down
To the streets of yonder town,
Where the people come and go,
Reap the harvest that they sow.

Like a field of wheat and tares,
Some are lost in worldly cares;
There are hearts as black as coal,
There are cripples of the soul.

Brothers, do not weep for me!
In His mercy I am free.
I can neither sow nor spin,
Yet, I am fed and clothed in Him.

I have been the donkey's tail,
Slower than a slug or snail;
You, my brothers, have been kind,
Never let me lag behind.

I have been most rich in friends,
You have been my feet and hands;
All the good that I could do,
I have done because of you.

    Oh my brothers, can't you see?
    You have been as Christ for me.
    And in my need I know I, too,
    Have become as Christ for you!

I have lived for forty years
In this wilderness of tears;
But these trials cannot compare
With the glory we will share.

I have had a voice to sing,
To rejoice in everything;
Now Love's sweet eternal song
Breaks the darkness with the dawn.

    Brothers, do not weep for me!
    Christ, the Lord, has set me free.
    Oh, my friends, remember this:
    Pain is not unhappiness.

Appendix
Prayers for the Journey of Life

The following is a little collection of prayers, some of them familiar and others quite unfamiliar, which have been helpful to the author of this book on the journey through life. They are presented for your meditation as they epitomize what I have tried to reflect in this book.

The Lord's Prayer
This is the best of all prayers. It is presented here with the meditations written by St. Francis of Assisi.

O OUR most holy FATHER,
Our Creator, Redeemer, Consoler, and Savior
WHO ARE IN HEAVEN:
In the angels and in the saints,
Enlightening them to love, because You, Lord, are light,
Inflaming them to love, because You, Lord, are love
Dwelling (in them) and filling them with happiness,
    because You, Lord, are the Supreme Good,
      the Eternal Good
   from Whom comes all good
   without Whom there is no good.

HALLOWED BE YOUR NAME:
May our knowledge of You become ever clearer
That we may know the breadth of Your blessings

the length of Your promises
the height of Your majesty
the depth of Your judgments.

YOUR KINGDOM COME:
So that You may rule in us through Your grace
and enable us to come to Your kingdom
    where there is an unclouded vision of You
        a perfect love of You
        a blessed companionship with You
        an eternal enjoyment of You.

YOUR WILL BE DONE ON EARTH AS IT IS IN
HEAVEN:
That we may love You with our whole heart by always
thinking of You
    with our whole soul by always desiring You
    with our whole mind by directing all our
        intentions to You and by seeking Your
        glory in everything
    and with our whole strength by spending all our
        energies and affections
        of soul and body
        in the service of Your love
        and of nothing else
and may we love our neighbors as ourselves
    by drawing them all with our whole strength to Your
        love
    by rejoicing in the good fortunes of others as well as
        our own
    and by sympathizing with the misfortunes of others
    and by giving offense to no one

GIVE US THIS DAY:
in memory and understanding and reverence
    of the love which (our Lord) Jesus Christ had for us
    and of those things which He said and did and
    suffered for us

OUR DAILY BREAD:
Your own Beloved Son, our Lord Jesus Christ

AND FORGIVE US OUR TRESPASSES:
Through Your ineffable mercy
through the power of the Passion of Your Beloved Son
    together with the merits and intercession of the
    Blessed Virgin
        Mary and all Your chosen ones

AS WE FORGIVE THOSE WHO TRESPASS AGAINST US:
And whatever we do not forgive perfectly,
do you, Lord, enable us to forgive to the full
so that we may truly love (our) enemies
and fervently intercede for them before You
returning no one evil for evil
and striving to help everyone in You.

AND LEAD US NOT INTO TEMPTATION
Hidden or obvious
Sudden or persistent

BUT DELIVER US FROM EVIL
Past, present, and to come.

Glory to the Father and to the Son and to the Holy Spirit
As it was in the beginning, is now, and will be forever.
Amen.[26]

A Universal Prayer (Attributed to Pope Clement XI)
This prayer is given in the back of the Sacramentary. It is
an excellent summary of developmental needs and potentials seen in the light of the Gospel.

Lord, I believe in you: increase my faith.
I trust in you: strengthen my trust.
I love you: let me love you more and more.
I am sorry for my sins: deepen my sorrow.

I worship you as my first beginning,
I long for you as my last end,
I praise you as my constant helper,
and call on you as my loving protector.

Guide me by your wisdom,
correct me with your justice,
comfort me with your mercy,
protect me with your power.

I offer you, Lord, my thoughts: to be fixed on you;
my words: to have you for their theme;
my actions: to reflect my love for you;
my sufferings: to be endured for your greater glory.

I want to do what you ask of me:
in the way you ask,
for as long as you ask,
because you ask it.

Lord, enlighten my understanding,
strengthen my will,
purify my heart,
and make me holy.

Help me to repent of my past sins
and to resist temptation in the future.
Help me to rise above my human weaknesses
and to grow stronger as a Christian.

Let me love you, my Lord and my God,
and see myself as I really am:
a pilgrim in this world,
a Christian called to respect and love
all whose lives I touch,
those in authority over me,
of those under my authority,
my friends and my enemies.

Help me to conquer anger with gentleness,
greed by generosity,
apathy by fervor.
Help me to forget myself
and reach out toward others.

Make me prudent in planning,
courageous in taking risks.
Make me patient in suffering, unassuming in prosperity.

Keep me, Lord, attentive at prayer,
temperate in food and drink,
diligent in my work,
firm in my good intentions.

Let my conscience be clear,
my conduct without fault,
my speech blameless,
my life well ordered.

Put me on guard against my human weaknesses.
Let me cherish your love for me,
keep your law,
and come at last to your salvation.

Teach me to realize that this world is passing,
that my true future is the happiness of heaven,
that life on earth is short,
and the life to come eternal.

Help me to prepare for death
with a proper fear of judgment,
but a greater trust in your goodness.
Lead me safely through death
to the endless joy of heaven.

Grant this through Christ our Lord. Amen.

A Simple Man's Prayer
The following verse was the only ornament in the room of
the Servant of God, Fr. Solanus Casey, a very humble and
simple Capuchin friar whose cause of beatification has been
presented to the Holy See:

BLESSED BE GOD IN ALL HIS DESIGNS

A Prayer When Things Go Well
The Twenty-Third Psalm
The LORD is my shepherd, I shall not want;
he makes me lie down in green pastures.
He leads me beside still waters;
he restores my soul.

He leads me in paths of righteousness
for his name's sake.

Even though I walk through the valley
of the shadow of death,
I fear no evil; for thou art with me;
thy rod and thy staff,
they comfort me.

Thou preparest a table before me
in the presence of my enemies;
thou anointest my head with oil,
my cup overflows.
Surely goodness and mercy shall follow me
all the days of my life;
and I shall dwell in the house of the LORD
for ever.

A Prayer in Darkness and Bitter Pain

The Eighty-Eighth Psalm
O LORD, my God, I call for help by day;
I cry out in the night before thee.
Let my prayer come before thee,
incline thy ear to my cry!

For my soul is full of troubles,
and my life draws near to Sheol.
I am reckoned among those who go
down to the Pit;
I am a man who has no strength,
like one forsaken among the dead,
like the slain that lie in the grave,
like those whom thou dost remember no more,
for they are cut off from thy hand.

Thou hast put me in the depths of
the Pit,
in the regions dark and deep.
Thy wrath lies heavy upon me,
and thou dost overwhelm me with
all thy waves.

Thou hast caused my companions to shun me;
thou hast made me a thing of
horror to them.
I am shut in so that I cannot escape;
my eye grows dim through sorrow.
Every day I call upon thee, O LORD;
I spread out my hands to thee.
Dost thou work wonders for the dead?
Do the shades rise up to praise thee?
Is thy steadfast love declared in the grave,
or thy faithfulness in Abaddon?
Are thy wonders known in the darkness,
or thy saving help in the land of
forgetfulness?

But I, O LORD, cry to thee;
in the morning my prayer comes
before thee.
O LORD, why dost thou cast me off?
Why dost thou hide thy face from me?
Afflicted and close to death from my
youth up,
I suffer thy terrors; I am helpless.
Thy wrath has swept over me;
thy dread assaults destroy me.
They surround me like a flood all day long;
they close in upon me together.

Thou hast caused lover and friend to shun me;
my companions are in darkness.

A Prayer in Uncertainty
John Henry Cardinal Newman
Lead Kindly Light

In 1833, after a voyage of several months through the Mediterranean, John Henry Newman, still an Anglican, turned homeward and embarked from Sicily on a vessel bound for Marseille. While becalmed off Sardinia in the Straits of Bonifacio, he composed a poem which he called "The Pillar of the Cloud," but which is universally known as "Lead Kindly Light."

Lead, Kindly Light, amid the encircling gloom
    Lead Thou me on!
The night is dark, and I am far from home—
    Lead Thou me on!
Keep Thou my feet; I do not ask to see
The distant scene—one step enough for me.

I was not ever thus, nor pray'd that Thou
    Shouldst lead me on.
I lov'd to choose and see my path; but now
    lead Thou me on!
I lov'd the garish day, and, spite of fears,
Pride rul'd my will; remember not past years.

So long Thy power hath bless'd me, sure it still
    Will lead me on,
O'er moor and fen, o'er crag and torrent, till
    The night is gone.
And with the morn those angel faces smile
Which I have lov'd long since, and lost awhile.

Prayer Against Foolishness
If ever, my God, it should happen through ignorance and passion that I persist in desires contrary to thine, may I be disappointed and punished, not by thy justice but by thy pity and great mercy.

Pere Jean-Pierre de Caussade

A Prayer to God All-Mighty and All-Wise
St. Augustine
This selection of verses is from the great prayer of St. Augustine contained in one of his earliest works, *The Soliloquies*. In this work the young convert was endeavoring to express the Christian doctrines of providence and trust.

O God, Founder of the universe, help me that I may pray aright,
    that I may act as one worthy to be heard by you and,
    finally, set me free.

God, to whom dissonance is nothing since, in the end, the
    worst resolves into harmony with the better.

God, whom every creature capable of loving, loves, whether
    consciously or unconsciously.

God, who does not permit any save the pure to know the true.

God, Father of truth
    Father of wisdom
    Father of the true and perfect life
    Father of blessedness
    Father of the good and beautiful
    Father of intelligible light
    Father of our awakening and enlightening
    Father of that pledge which warns us to return to you!

God, whose kingdom is that whole realm unknown to sense:
    from whose kingdom law for even these lower
      realms is derived;

from whom to turn is to fall;
to whom to turn is to rise;
in whom to abide is to stand secure;
from whom to depart is to waste away;
to whom to return is to be restored to life;
in whom to dwell is to live;
whom no one, unless deceived, loses;
whom no one, unless stirred to do so, seeks;
whom no one, unless purified, finds.

God, to whom faith urges; hope uplifts; love joins.

God, through whom we overcome the enemy,

    You do I supplicate!

God, whose gift it is that we do not utterly perish;
  by whom we are warned to watch.

God, through whom we discriminate good things from evil things;
  through whom we flee from evil and follow after good.

God, through whom we yield not to adversity;
  through whom we both serve well and rule well;
  through whom we discern that certain things we had deemed
    essential to ourselves are truly foreign to us,
    while those things that we deemed foreign to us
    are essential.

God, through whom we are not held fast by the baits and seductions
    of the wicked;
  through whom the decrease of our possessions does not
    diminish us;
  through whom death is swallowed up in victory.

God, who makes us worthy of being heard;
  who defends us;
  who leads us into all truth;
  who speaks all good things to us!

God, who recalls us to the path;
    who leads us to the door and opens it to those who knock;
    who gives us the bread of life.

God, through whom we thirst for that water because of which, having
    drunk, we shall never thirst again,
    who purifies and prepares us for divine rewards,
                                        come to me!

In whatever I say, come to my help, O you one God,
    in whom there is all steadfastness, abundance, and life;
    where nothing is lacking and nothing redundant;
    by whose laws the universe is perfectly ordered;
    by whose laws the will of the soul is free.

God, above whom, outside of whom, without whom is nothing;
    beneath whom, in whom, with whom is everything.

God, who made man after your own image and likeness,
                        hear me, my God, my all, hear me!

    Open my ears that I may hear your commands;
    Open my eyes that I may see your nod,
    Cast all unsoundness from me that I may recognize you!

Tell me where to direct my gaze that I may look upon you,
    and I hope that I shall do all things which you command!

Let your door be open to my knock, and teach me how to come
    to you.

I have nothing other than your will,
    I know nothing other than that the fleeting and the falling
        should be spurned;
        the fixed and eternal sought after.

I know not how to make my way to you—suggest it, make it plain, equip
    me for the journey.

If they who take refuge in you find you
>> by faith, give me faith
>> by virtue, give me virtue
>> by knowledge, give me knowledge.

Increase my faith, increase my hope, increase my charity.

After you I am groping, and by whatever things you may be felt after,
even these do I seek from you!
> For if you desert a man, he perishes; but you desert him not,
> for you are the sum of good, and no man, seeking you aright,
> has failed to find you; and every one seeks you aright whom you
> cause so to seek you.

> Cause me, O Father, to seek you; let me not stray from the path, and
> to me, seeking you, let nothing befall in place of yourself!

> If I desire nothing beside yourself, let me, I implore, find you now;
> but if there is in me the desire for something beside yourself, do
> you yourself purify me, and make me fit to look upon you!

For the rest,
> whatever concerns the welfare of this mortal body of mine, so
> long as I do not know how it may serve either myself or those I
> love, to you, Father, wisest and best, do I commit it, and I
> pray that you will admonish me concerning it as shall be
> needful.

But this I do implore your most excellent mercy,

> that you convert me in my inmost self to you, and, as I incline
> toward you, let nothing oppose;

> command that so long as I endure and care for this same body, I
> may be pure and magnanimous and just and prudent, a perfect lover
> and learner of your wisdom, a fit inhabitant of a dwelling place
> in your most blessed kingdom!

Amen and Amen!

A Philosopher's Prayer
O Father, give the spirit power to climb
To the fountain of all light, and be purified.
Break through the mists of earth, the weight of the clod,
Shine forth in splendor, Thou that art calm weather,
And quiet resting place for faithful souls.
To see Thee is the end and the beginning,
Thou carriest us, and Thou dost go before,
Thou art the journey, and the journey's end.

Boethius—sixth century Christian philosopher
(translation by Helen Waddell)[27]

A Healer's Prayer
I begin once more my daily work. Be thou with me, Almighty Father of Mercy, in all my efforts to heal the sick. For without thee, man is but a helpless creature. Grant that I may be filled with love for my art and for my fellow-men. May the thirst for gain and the desire for fame be far from my heart. For these are the enemies of pity and the ministers of hate. Grant that I may be able to devote myself, body and soul, to thy children who suffer from pain.

Preserve my strength, that I may be able to restore the strength of the rich and the poor, the good and the bad, the friend and the foe. Let me see in the sufferer the man alone. When wiser men teach me, let me be humble to learn, for the mind of man is so puny and the art of healing is so vast. But when fools are ready to advise me or to find fault with me, let me not listen to their folly. Let me be intent upon one thing, O Father of Mercy—to be always merciful to thy suffering children.

May there never rise in me the notion that I know enough, but give me the strength and leisure and zeal to enlarge my knowledge. Our work is great, and the mind of man presses forward forever. Thou hast chosen me in thy grace, to watch over the life and death of thy creatures. I am about to fulfill my duties; guide me in this immense work so that it may be of avail.

> *Moses Maimonides*—twelfth century
> Jewish philosopher, theologian, and physician

A Prayer in the Face of Death
Give me thy grace, good Lord,
To set the world at nought,
To set my mind fast upon thee,
And not to hang upon the blast of men's mouths.
To be content to be solitary.
Not to long for worldly company,
Little and little utterly to cast off the world,
And rid my mind of all the business thereof.
Not to long to hear of any worldly things,
But that the hearing of worldly phantasies
     may be to me displeasant.
Gladly to be thinking of God,
Piteously to call for his help
To lean unto the comfort of God,
Busily to labor to love him.
To know mine own vility and wretchedness,
To humble and meeken myself under
     the mighty hand of God,
To bewail my sins passed,
For the purging of them, patiently
     to suffer adversity.
Gladly to bear my purgatory here,
To be joyful of tribulations,
To walk the narrow way that leadeth to life.

To bear the cross with Christ,
To have the last thing in remembrance.
To have ever afore mine eye my death
    that is ever at hand,
To make death no stranger to me
To foresee and consider the everlasting
    fire of hell,
To pray for pardon before the judge come.
To have continually in mind the passion
    that Christ suffered for me.
For his benefits uncessantly to give him thanks.
To buy the time again that I before have lost.
To abstain from vain confabulations,
To eschew light foolish mirth and gladness,
Recreations not necessary to cut off.
Of worldly substance, friends, liberty, life
    and all, to set the loss at right nought,
    for the winning of Christ.
To think my most enemies my best friends,
For the the brethren of Joseph could never have
    done him so much good with their love and favor
    as they did him with their malice and hatred.
These minds are more to be desired of every man
    than all the treasure of all the princes and
    kings, Christian and heathen,
    were it gathered and laid together all upon one heap.

Written in 1534 by St. Thomas More
while a prisoner in the Tower of
London awaiting execution

Prayer to Our Lady in the Sorrow of Life
Hail, holy Queen, Mother of mercy,
Hail, our life, our sweetness
        and our hope!
To you do we cry,
Poor banished children of Eve!
To you do we send up our sighs,
        mourning and weeping
        in this vale of tears.
Turn then, most gracious advocate,
Your eyes of mercy toward us;
And, after this our exile, show us
        the blessed fruit of your womb,
        Jesus.
O clement, O loving, O sweet Virgin Mary!
Pray for us, O holy Mother of God,
That we may be made worthy of the
        promises of Christ.

Blessed Herman of Reichenau, O.S.B.

Notes

1. Cf. Romans 5:12–14; Council of Trent, Session 5, June 17, 1546, *Decree on Original Sin;* Pope Paul VI, *The Creed of the People of God,* June 30, 1968; Vatican II, Pastoral Constitution on the Church in the Modern World (Gaudium et Spes) December 7, 1965, no. 12–14. *The Teaching of Christ,* ed. Ronald Lawler and Donald Wuerl (Huntington, Indiana: O.S.V. Press, 1983) pp. 71–72.

2. *National Review,* June 11, 1982, p. 677. Article by Thomas Molnar.

3. Thomas Merton, *The Waters of Siloe* (New York: Harcourt Brace, 1949).

4. Matthew Linn, S.J., and Dennis Linn, S.J., *Deliverance Prayer* (New York: Paulist Press, 1980).

5. *Liturgy of the Hours* (New York: Catholic Book Publishing Company, 1975), 11th Week in Ordinary Time, p. 376.

6. *National Review,* loc. cit.

7. *Psychology Today,* Vol. 17, no. 9 September 1983, p. 25.

8. *Ibid.,* p. 30.

9. St. John of the Cross, *The Collected Works,* ed. Kieran Kavanaugh, O.C.D., and Otilio Rodriguez, O.C.D. (Washington, D.C.: ICS Publications, 1973), Book II, Chapter 6, p. 88.

10. *Op. cit.,* pp. 110–113.

11. Romano Guardini, *The Lord* (Chicago: Henry Regnery Company, 1978). Chapter 3, pp. 13–18.

12. *Treasury of Traditional Wisdom,* ed. Withall Perry (New York: Simon and Schuster, 1971), p. 501.

13. *Ibid.,* p. 504.

14. St. Francis de Sales, letter cited in *The Soul Afire,* ed., H. A. Reinhold (New York: Doubleday Image Books, 1973), p. 104.

15. St. John of the Cross, *op. cit.,* p. 699.

16. Jean-Pierre de Caussade, *Abandonment to Divine Providence* (New York: Doubleday Image Books, 1966).

17. Blessed Julian of Norwich, *Enfolded in Love,* ed. Rev. Robert Llewellyn (London: Darton, Longman & Todd, 1980), p. 39.

18. Sister Audrey Marie Detiege, *Henriette de Lisle, Free Woman of Color* (Sisters of the Holy Family, 6901 Chef Menteur Highway, New Orleans, Louisiana 70120, 1976).

19. *Liturgy of the Hours, op. cit.,* I, January 5, p. 1692.

20. Matthew Linn, S.J. and Dennis Linn, S.J., *Healing of Memories* (New York: Paulist Press, 1984).

21. Francois de Salignac de la Mothe Fenelon, *The Royal Way of the Cross* (Orleans, Maine: Paraclete Press, 1982), pp. 145–146.

22. There are many fine biographies of St. Francis. One of the most factual is Johannes Jorgensen's *St. Francis of Assisi* (New York: Doubleday Image Books, 1955).

23. Margaret T. Munro, *The Ragged Saint* (Houston: Lumen Christi). The text of this book is taken from Margaret Munro's *A Book of Unlikely Saints* (London: 1943, by permission of the Longman Group Limited).

24. Cited in *The Soul Afire,* ed. H. A. Reinhold (New York: Doubleday Image Books, 1973), p. 146.

25. Copyright William Barton Hurlburt, M.D., Woodside Music, Box 620-400, Woodside, California 94062, August 1983.

26. *Francis and Clare. The Complete Works.* Translated by Regis Armstrong, OFM Cap., and Ignatius Brady, OFM (New York: Paulist Press, 1982).

27. Cited in *More Latin Lyrics, from Virgil to Milton,* translated by Helen Waddell, ed. D. Felicitas Corrigan, OSB. (London: Gollancz, 1976), p. 113.